The Real Queen of Hearts Ain't Even Pretty

A Play in Two Acts

Brad Bailey

A Samuel French Acting Edition

SAMUEL
FRENCH
FOUNDED 1830

SAMUELFRENCH.COM
SAMUELFRENCH-LONDON.CO.UK

FOR PRODUCTION ENQUIRIES

UNITED STATES AND CANADA
Info@SamuelFrench.com
1-866-598-8449

UNITED KINGDOM AND EUROPE
Plays@SamuelFrench-London.co.uk
020-7255-4302

Each title is subject to availability from Samuel French, depending upon country of performance. Please be aware that *THE REAL QUEEN OF HEARTS AIN'T EVEN PRETTY* may not be licensed by Samuel French in your territory. Professional and amateur producers should contact the nearest Samuel French office or licensing partner to verify availability.

MUSIC USE NOTE

Licensees are solely responsible for obtaining formal written permission from copyright owners to use copyrighted music in the performance of this play and are strongly cautioned to do so. If no such permission is obtained by the licensee, then the licensee must use only original music that the licensee owns and controls. Licensees are solely responsible and liable for all music clearances and shall indemnify the copyright owners of the play(s) and their licensing agent, Samuel French, against any costs, expenses, losses and liabilities arising from the use of music by licensees. Please contact the appropriate music licensing authority in your territory for the rights to any incidental music.

IMPORTANT BILLING AND CREDIT REQUIREMENTS

If you have obtained performance rights to this title, please refer to your licensing agreement for important billing and credit requirements.

THE REAL QUEEN OF HEARTS AIN'T EVEN PRET-
TY had its world premiere at The University of Alabama's Allen Bales Theatre on December 1, 1982. It was
directed by Jeff West and the cast was as follows:

LIZ NICHOLS. Sandra Mitchell
CASS WILSON. . . . . Jeanna Lankford
SHERRI LEE SPEER. . . . . Kris Prunitsch
PAULA BURGESS . . . . Drew Penick

The first professional production of the play opened in
Los Angeles at The Actors Playhouse on October 13,
1983, presented by Epra, Inc. in association with Ken
Harris, Ray Laurent and Brad Nye. It was directed by Jeff
West with lighting by Joe Fitzpatrick and costumes by
Will Rowe. The cast was as follows:

LIZ NICHOLS. . . . . Patricia Murray
CASS WILSON . . . . Sherry Willis-Burch
SHERRI LEE SPEER. . . . . Kathleen York
PAULA BURGESS . . . . Irene Arranga

CHARACTERS

LIZ NICHOLS — *eighteen years old, Liz is bright, funny, attractive enough to have been First Alternate in the Queen of Hearts Pageant the year before. Very ambitious, Liz can best be described as a leader, a mover and shaper. Along with these qualities of leadership comes the ability to manipulate others to her advantage. These machinations are nothing major, just harmless, high school games. She is head cheerleader at WCHS and very popular with her classmates, but Liz doesn't find any of this very substantial. Of the four girls, she is definitely the most future-oriented.*

CASS WILSON — *eighteen years old, Cass is an incurable follower. Average intelligence and average looks, but she wants the beauty, the glamour that she knows is out of reach but attainable through others. Liz is everything that Cass wants to be. Cass is firmly rooted in the present, very wrapped up in school activities. The uncertainty of the future frightens her. In order to avoid peer harrassment, Cass is always ready to ridicule the nearest scapegoat, anyone she feels is inferior to herself.*

SHERRI LEE SPEER — *eighteen years old, Sherri Lee moved to Double Springs the previous summer and began her senior year at WCHS. She is a "classic beauty" and would almost have to be tall and blonde. She has no friends — the girls resent her and the boys are intimidated by her. Though she seems a caricatured "bitch-goddess" initially, we soon see there is much more underneath that exterior. Unlike Liz, though, her manipulatory tactics are highly honed and practiced. There is a reason for everything she does.*

PAULA BURGESS — *eighteen years old, Paula is neither popular nor unpopular. At WCHS, she has always been "on the fringe," taken for granted, or worse, ignored. There is a touch of the innocent babe in her make-up, ultimately appealing in its way. For all her funny stories and "out of the blue" proclamations, there is something disturbing about Paula. She doesn't know it yet, but she is one of the defeated.*

PLACE

The Winston County High School gymnasium in Double Springs, Alabama (Pop. 980, approx.)

SETTING

The girl's locker room at the WCHS gym, backstage of the annual Queen of Hearts beauty pageant, which is already in progress.

TIME

The Saturday night before Easter Sunday, 1976.

ACT ONE

Evening. Around 8:45 pm.

ACT TWO

That same evening. One hour later.

THE REAL QUEEN OF HEARTS AIN'T EVEN PRETTY

ACT ONE

SCENE: We see the girls' locker room at Winston County High School. This is probably not the main locker room and is now used more for storage than anything else. The setting should suggest this.

This room has, for the night, been converted into a dressing room for the girls who are contestants in the annual Queen of Hearts Beauty Pageant.

The walls are of institutional concrete block, painted perhaps dark grey from floor level up to three feet, then the paint might be of a lighter grey shade.

The room could conceivably be a sort of "halfway point" between the shower room and the gymnasium. There should be some suggestion that there are showers in the next room, and this could be done with a door leading offstage at extreme stage left. The same should apply with a door at stage right leading offstage into the gymnasium, where we are told the actual pageant is now in progress. On the wall through which this doorway leads, there is an electrical switch and wallplate. This switch is responsible for turning the locker

*room lights on and off. It will be used twice in the course of
the play. Also, when the locker room lights are switched off,
there should be just enough spill light through the doorway to
subtly illuminate the action onstage.*

*Upstage center is a row of old, rusty lockers (actually a
double-row, stacked one on top of the other. These lockers
were probably shunted off into this room when new lockers
were installed in the shower room.) Resting on top of the
lockers are cardboard boxes bearing magic-marker inscrip-
tions, "Flags," "Hats," etc. From a box marked "Cheerleaders" we see a pair of purple and gold pom-pons
spilling out.*

*A long table, piled high with make-up paraphernalia is in
front of the lockers, leaving enough space for walking between the two.*

*Somewhere in the room we might see a water fountain,
similar to those found in schools everywhere. It is not
necessary that the fountain be functional, though that would
be a nice piece of business. Still, this prop is optional.*

*Downstage right and left are small tables with a chair each.
These are used as dressing tables for the contestants. They
could possibly have mirrors attached, but as this tends to
block view, perhaps small lighted make-up mirrors should be
used, the type with adjustments for various lighting choices
— a regular mirror on one side and a magnifying mirror on
the other.*

Scattered about on these tables are the endless cosmetic "tools of the trade" — myriads of lipsticks, nail polishes, powders, creams, on and on and on. Also, on the table at stage right is a blow-dryer, one of those models that somewhat resemble a ray-gun used in low-budget sci-fi movies.

Centerstage, running from downstage to up, are two low benches parallel to one another. They are painted the same color as the upper portion of the wall.

Somewhere between the lockers upstage and the downstage left dressing table is a large cardboard refrigerator crate, nearly six feet high. It should not be all that obvious, with the other boxes around.

Small overnight cases should be here and there, along with several garment bags. Discarded clothes are on the floor, others hang from any available place. Used tissues litter the area, along with fast-food sacks and cups.

In short, the room is pretty much trashed. Imagine that forty high school girls have been running amuck for a couple of hours and you'll get a fairly accurate idea of this battlefield.

AT RISE: At the table downstage left, LIZ NICHOLS is applying her fourth or fifth shade of borrowed lipstick. She is dressed very casually in a man's shirt and bell-bottomed jeans. Also tennis shoes.

CASS WILSON, Liz's best friend, is also onstage. She is dressed in jeans and a faded sweatshirt with "WCHS" in large letters across the front and "Pep Squad" in smaller letters across the back. CASS is straddling the bench nearest LIZ, a deck of playing cards in a solitaire pattern spread on the bench between her legs.

LIZ. *(applying the lipstick)* ...And nobody could believe it when she won Queen of Hearts that year.

CASS. What year?

LIZ. The year Connie and them graduated. 1969. Yeah, Sharon Porter was Queen of Hearts in '69.

CASS. I heard it was just a joke.

LIZ. No. It was real!

CASS. But Sharon Porter?

LIZ. Yeah. *(Takes the lipstick from her lips.)* Everybody used to call her Sharon Pooter. *(Makes a flatulent noise with her newly-painted lips.)*

CASS. *(Laughs.)* God. What kinda judges did they *have* back then?

LIZ. Weren't any judges. I mean, there were judges, but not like out there. *(Indicates offstage right.)* Back then, the contest wasn't a beautywalk or anything like now.

CASS. Surely to God she wasn't elected.

LIZ. Naw. It was because of her class picture.

CASS. You're kidding.

LIZ. Nope. They got all the girls in the school to submit a picture and then sent 'em off somewhere to be judged.

CASS. Who by?

LIZ. That year it was some people at Southern Living

Magazine. They just picked the girl that looked the best in her picture.

CASS. *Sharon Porter?*

LIZ. I don't know how, but her picture was beautiful. I mean it. They took it through a smudged lens or something.

CASS. *Real* smudged.

LIZ. It looked real glamorous—like a movie star or something.

CASS. Southern Living Magazine?

LIZ. Yep.

CASS. What do they know about a beauty contest?

LIZ. I saw in a old yearbook where one time they sent the pictures out to Hollywood to be judged.

CASS. *(dreamily)* Hollywood.

LIZ. That year, Queen of Hearts was picked by—are you ready? Tiny Tim and Miss Vicki.

CASS. God.

LIZ. *Tiny Tim and Miss Vicki!* And then one year, they sent all the pictures down to Montgomery and the Young Democrats picked the winner.

CASS. Who'd they pick?

LIZ. *(Laughs.)* Rita Woods.

CASS. Rita Woods!

LIZ. *(offhand.)* Yeah. Everybody said she won just because she looked so much like George Wallace. Except for the mustache.

CASS. He hasn't got a mustache.

LIZ. I was talking about *Rita.*

CASS. *(laughing)* You're crazy!

LIZ. *(grandly)* And that's the reason for all *this* mess.

Because you can't judge beauty from pictures. So they decided to make it a beautywalk.

CASS. *(pointing to lipstick)* Whose is that?

LIZ. Nancy Noblett's. *(turning from mirror to face CASS)* What do you think?

CASS. Umm. I don't know.

LIZ. I think it's too much.

CASS. Yeah. Too much. *(Points to an elaborate evening gown hanging prominently nearby.)* Who's wearing this?

LIZ. Nobody. It's Sherri Lee's. She decided to wear something else.

CASS. Again?

LIZ. Yeah. Again. *(Beat)* After I already spit on it and everything. *(CASS laughs again.)* I really wanted to kill her last night.

CASS. When?

LIZ. *(crossing to CASS)* At rehearsal last night. Well, her old mother, too. Dragging in six suits for streetwear and four gowns. *(She jumps up on the bench and mimicks.)* "I want to see which one looks the best under the lights. Sherri Lee has such delicate coloring and all, I want to pick just the right shade" — *(dropping her pose)* Shit. I just can't believe Sherri Lee's in this contest.

CASS. Everybody hates her guts.

LIZ. The boys don't. They think she's something great. I thought it was kinda funny when all the clubs elected girls to be in Queen of Hearts. Sherri Lee was nominated in every club—by the *boys*—but the *girls* always voted her out. Beta Club, F.T.A., Library Club, same thing. The boys would nominate her and the girls would vote for *anybody* else but Sherri Lee.

CASS. *(matter-of-factly)* Well she's in the contest.

Liz. We ran out of girls!

Cass. You got nominated. You turned it down.

Liz. Last year was enough for me. Anyway, no girls were left and Sherri Lee *had* to get in. But she was the last one. How do you think Diane Batson got in? *(With her arms she indicates DIANE's size.)*

Cass. God.

Liz. I mean, I like Diane and all, but she's no beauty. She's so fat, she can't get school insurance to cover her.

Cass. Really?

Liz. And in P.E., they won't let her get *near* the trampoline. Everybody else is jumping up and down on the trampoline and there's Diane, way over yonder, jumping on a wrestling mat.

Cass. God, Liz.

Liz. Yeah, we did a real good job of keeping Sherri Lee out of the contest—us girls did.

Cass. Until Ag Class.

Liz. Those stupid-ass boys. I could kill 'em every one.

Cass. I know it.

Liz. They think Sherri Lee's such a sweet little thing. Just because she's the new girl in school. You know how she acts around boys.

Cass. Stupid-ass boys.

Liz. She's such a damned goody-goody. Miss Head Majorette—Miss Feature Twirler. And she's engaged. Or she says she is. Why do the boys like her? She's getting married.

Cass. She's such a goody-goody.

LIZ. Can't you just hear her in her interview tonight? I bet she really slobbered all over those judges. *(mimicking)* "My name's Sherri Lee Speer, and I'm representing the Future Farmers of America. My hobbies are sign language, reading to shut-ins, and praying a lot. In my spare time, I'm a volunteer seeing-eye person for blind dogs."

CASS. *(howling)* You're crazy!

LIZ. All I can say is, she's in pretty bad shape when she's the last girl in the whole school to get picked for Queen of Hearts.

CASS. *(seriously)* I didn't get picked.

LIZ. Well, yeah ... but ... you didn't want to, remember? I asked you to help me back here. You didn't wanna be in that shitty contest.

CASS. Yes, I did.

LIZ. No, you didn't.

CASS. I kinda did.

LIZ. You're not missing a thing.

CASS. You were in it last year.

LIZ. Big deal.

CASS. First alternate.

LIZ. Big deal.

CASS. It *is* a big deal. You could've won it too—if you'da tried. *(LIZ laughs.)* Well, you *could've*. But no, you go out there in evening wear chewing on a wad of gum as big as my fist.

LIZ. *(Laughs.)* I forgot to spit it out.

CASS. You did not. You did it on purpose.

LIZ. *(grinning)* No, I didn't.

CASS. Liz, you blew a bubble a foot wide.

Liz. *(mock-indignation) I did not.*

Cass. There's a picture in the yearbook.

Liz. Oh, yeah.

Cass. "Oh yeah"—and you coulda *won* it too, Liz, if—

Liz. God, Cass, you act like it's the damned Miss America Pageant or something. It's no big deal.

Cass. It is *here.*

Liz. My God, yes! Such an honor! They throw a dozen half-dead roses in your hands and stick a tacky little crown on your head and push you out front, and you walk around the gym and people clap and yell and whistle—and old men squint at your tits—and you smile, but just a little, or your gums'll show in all the pictures—and you cry, but just a little, or your mascara'll run, and all the time, Eddie Akers is singing into a microphone: *(She strikes a hammy pose and sings.)* "So meet the lovely Queen of Hearts..."

Cass. *(laughing)* He's such a queer.

Liz. Who's a queer?

Cass. Eddie Akers.

Liz. He is not.

Cass. *(proof positive)* Liz, he wears an *I.D. bracelet.*

Liz. So what?

Cass. And he's always messing with the girls' hair.

Liz. Cass, if he was a queer, he'd be messing with the *boys'* hair.

Cass. Well, maybe he does.

Liz. He does not. And he's *not* a queer.

Cass. *(walking away)* Well, if I'd know you were in *love* with Eddie Akers, I never woulda mentioned it.

LIZ. I'm not in *love* with Eddie Akers.

CASS. He's always hanging around you. He's in love with you. I think he's sickening.

LIZ. *(enjoying this)* You're jealous. You're jealous, but who of? Me or Eddie?

CASS. I'm not jealous! I just hate him, that's all.

LIZ. *(craftily)* He likes you.

CASS. Bull.

LIZ. He drew that picture of you.

CASS. I know it.

LIZ. And he had it framed, too.

CASS. I know it.

LIZ. He has a crush on you.

CASS. *God.*

LIZ. He's kinda cute, too. I think. Don't you think he's cute?

CASS. Cute?

LIZ. Yeah. Yeah, I think he's cute. Don't you think he's cute?

CASS. Well, I guess—in a ugly sort of way.

LIZ. Would you go to the prom with him?

CASS. NO WAY! *(then, hopefully)* Do you think maybe he might ask me?

LIZ. He'll ask you.

CASS. How do you know?

LIZ. I just know.

CASS. *(suspiciously)* Did you tell Eddie Akers to ask me?

LIZ. No, I *paid* him to ask you!

CASS. LIZ!

LIZ. Not really.

Cass. Did he tell you to ask me?

Liz. No.

Cass. Then why did you say that?

Liz. *(candidly)* Do you have a date for the prom?

Cass. Do *you?*

Liz. Yes.

Cass. You didn't tell me. Who with?

Liz. Greg.

Cass. Greg *Atkins?*

Liz. Yeah.

Cass. *Why?*

Liz. Why not?

Cass. But Tony asked you. And Rob did, too.

Liz. Football players.

Cass. So?

Liz. I don't date football players.

Cass. *You're* head cheerleader.

Liz. And everybody knows cheerleaders date football players. Well, I don't.

Cass. But Greg Atkins?

Liz. Greg's a genius. He's gonna be Valedictorian and everything.

Cass. But nobody likes him.

Liz. I do.

Cass. But he doesn't play football or anything.

Liz. That's right, Cass. And because he doesn't have a neck like a tree trunk and sweat like a pig, the hicks here don't like him.

Cass. *I* don't like him.

Liz. Well, you're not going to the prom with him, either.

CASS. And I wouldn't, either.

LIZ. You'd go with anybody that'd ask you.

CASS. I would not.

LIZ. You sure are picky for somebody who doesn't have a date. You don't have a date, do you?

CASS. Why do you think I don't?

LIZ. 'Cause if you did, youda written his name all over your notebooks.

CASS. Well.

LIZ. *(enthusiastically)* I told Eddie Akers to ask you.

CASS. *(walking away)* No thanks.

LIZ. Why not?

CASS. I don't want a date.

LIZ. You're not going to our Senior Prom?

CASS. I'm going. I just don't want a date.

LIZ. *Everybody* wants a date.

CASS. *(resentfully)* You've changed *your* mind.

LIZ. Changed my mind?

CASS. About the prom. Us going together.

LIZ. Oh.

CASS. It's what you said.

LIZ. Cass...

CASS. You *said*. You said we'd go together—just me and you—we'd get drunk as hell and go to the prom.

LIZ. *(ashamed)* I know.

CASS. But that was before *you* had a date.

LIZ. Cass.

CASS. It doesn't matter. I don't care.

LIZ. You're mad. *(Beat)* Cass, we'll see each other there—at the prom. *(Silence. LIZ crosses to table, gets brush and hesitantly begins to brush CASS' ponytail. She tries to lighten*

the mood.) Hey. Did you see how drunk Debbie was?
Huh?

CASS. *(Mumbles.)* Yeah.

LIZ. She's really drunk. I had to do her make-up for
her. She kept poking herself in the eyeball with the mascara. *(This gets a stifled smile from CASS.)* Hey. They drank
four bottles of Boone's Farm.

CASS. *(succumbing to LIZ's charm)* What kind?

LIZ. Strawberry Hill.

CASS. Who?

LIZ. Her and Sara.

CASS. God.

LIZ. Last year, I was so drunk, I couldn't see.

CASS. Really?

LIZ. Uh huh. And Phyllis and them had some pot.

CASS. *(shocked)* Pot? *Marijuana?*

LIZ. Yeah.

CASS. Here at school?

LIZ. Yeah.

CASS. You couldn't tell.

LIZ. Tell what?

CASS. That you were drunk or — *stoned.* You acted
normal. Except for when you blew the bubble. You
couldn't tell.

LIZ. *I* could tell. *(still brushing)* Hey. You know
Cindy?

CASS. Yeah.

LIZ. Last year Cindy smoked some dope right before
she had to go down for her interview with the judges.

CASS. What happened?

LIZ. She disappeared! Nobody could find her and the

judges were calling her number.

Cass. God.

Liz. People were looking for her everywhere. I finally found her. Up in the bandroom.

Cass. In the bandroom?

Liz. Behind the sousaphone. She was a mess.

Cass. What did you do?

Liz. Walked her around a little and then sent her on down to the judges.

Cass. She went to the interview? Like that?

Liz. *(matter-of-factly)* That's the whole *point* of the thing, Cass.

Cass. What?

Liz. To see how messed up you can get and still *do it* — be in the contest.

Cass. Oh.

Liz. Those interviews are so stupid, anyway. They ask you things like "Why do you want to be Queen of Hearts?" and "If you had one wish, what would it be?"

Cass. God. How stupid.

Liz. Yeah. And Cindy gets in there *somehow* and sits down in front of the judges. And some old lady judge with like, blue hair and cat-eye glasses, looks at Cindy and says — *(a nasal voice)* "Tell us, Miss, about your hobbies." And Cindy leans over the table and goes — *(Theme music for "The Twilight Zone."*)*

Do do do do,

Do do do do ... *(They both laugh loudly.)*

---

* Cautionary Note: Permission to produce this play does *not* include permission to use this music in production.

CASS. *(still laughing)* Hey, Liz?

LIZ. *(laughing)* Huh?

CASS. I don't get it.

LIZ. Neither do I, but it was great! *(laughing)* And Cindy still got in the top ten!

CASS. Is anybody messed up tonight?

LIZ. Not like that. Well, I don't know. I was too busy trying to get 'em ready. *(She looks at SHERRI LEE's gown.)* You know what?

CASS. What?

LIZ. I'd love to see Sherri Lee stoned.

CASS. Yeah. That would be fun. *(Beat. Then CASS sings.)*

Do do do do,

Do do do do ... *(CASS laughs. LIZ stares at the gown.)*

LIZ. You think she'll win?

CASS. Do you?

LIZ. She's got a good chance.

CASS. Donna might win.

LIZ. Yeah, Donna's pretty, but did you see her *dress?*

CASS. Yeah.

LIZ. That's about the ugliest dress I've ever seen on a human. Looked like it was made by Helen Keller.

CASS. Donna said *she* made it.

LIZ. I know, but she shouldn't admit it. She ought to say her *mother* made it.

CASS. She thought it would impress the judges if they knew she made it herself.

LIZ. It will—if she walks out there with a German Shepherd and a white cane.

(SHERRI LEE enters, wearing a formal evening gown. A heart-shaped piece of paper with the number "13"—in silver glitter—is pinned to her gown at mid-thigh.)

CASS. *(Not seeing SHERRI LEE.)* It sure was ugly.

SHERRI LEE. It sure *was.*

CASS. Huh?

SHERRI LEE. You said Donna's dress was ugly. I think so, too.

LIZ. How long have you been listening?

SHERRI LEE. Hey Liz, that was pretty funny what you said about—

LIZ. You can't come in here, Sherri Lee.

SHERRI LEE. Mrs. Taylor said I could.

CASS. How long you been out there listening?

SHERRI LEE. Long enought. Liz—

LIZ. You gotta have a pass, Sherri Lee.

SHERRI LEE. I need my earrings. I forgot to put them on.

LIZ. You forgot your pass, too.

SHERRI LEE. *(pointing to dresser top)* Well, *there they are.* Hiding from me. If they'd been a snake, they'd a just bit me.

LIZ. Don't flatter yourself.

SHERRI LEE. That's what I came after. *(She begins to cross. LIZ steps between SHERRI LEE and the earrings.)*

LIZ. A pass, Sherri Lee—

SHERRI LEE. But Mrs. Taylor told me—

LIZ. Mrs. Taylor told *me* that nobody gets in without a pass. Do you have a pass?

SHERRI LEE. *(irritated)* No, I do not.

Liz. *(Shrugs to CASS, who returns the shrug.)* You need a pass.

Sherri Lee. *(sugary)* Now Liz, let's not be silly about this. *(She starts for the earrings, but LIZ stops her.)* Cassie, would you please hand me those earrings there? *(CASS moves toward dresser. LIZ, without turning to see, points behind herself at CASS.)*

Liz. Stop! *(Beat)* Sherri Lee, do you know why *we're* back here?

Sherri Lee. *(gleefully wicked)* Well, I guess because *we're* not in the pageant.

Liz. *(to CASS:)* Smart girl. *(back to SHERRI LEE:)* And do you know *why* we're not in the pageant?

Sherri Lee. Well, I guess because you couldn't get nominated.

Cass. We got nomina — *(She trails off, then:)* Liz got nominated.

Liz. We're here, Sherri Lee, because last year — *(She advances toward SHERRI LEE as she speaks, backing her up a bit. CASS follows behind LIZ.)* —when everybody was out *there,* somebody got back *here* and stole money, and jewelry, and clothes. If we weren't here now, your earrings might not be here, either. Now I told Mrs. Taylor I'd do this and Cass said she'd help me. We're here, Sherri Lee, so what happened last year won't happen again. *Now* do you see?

Sherri Lee. *(smiling)* Ohhh. And I thought it was because y'all are so *homely.*

Cass. *(Steps forward, speaking sugary at first.)* Get the shit outta here, Sherri Lee. Get the shit outta here before I slap your TITS UP AROUND YOUR EARS! *(SHERRI*

LEE is near the door.)

SHERRI LEE. I'm telling Mrs. Taylor what you said. She doesn't like cussing.

CASS. *(advancing, then lunging)* Well I didn't cuss, YOU STUPID BITCH!

SHERRI LEE. *(Exiting)* MRS. TAYLOR! *(Beat)*

LIZ. I'm glad you didn't lose your cool, Cass.

CASS. *(fuming and stomping toward table)* That bitch! I hate that bitch!

LIZ. She'll come back.

CASS. *(Grabs earrings.)* Well, she won't get these.

LIZ. What you gonna do? Eat 'em?

CASS. NO. I'M NOT GONNA ... *(Stops, then laughs.)* No.

LIZ. *(taking earrings and dangling them)* These are kinda floozy for Little Miss Bible School.

CASS. You think they're real?

LIZ. Real glass.

CASS. She's got a diamond ring.

LIZ. It's little. I bet he couldn't afford a big one.

CASS. She's not gonna marry him, anyway.

LIZ. How do *you* know?

CASS. She told me.

LIZ. *(mock delight)* Ohhh. I didn't know y'all talked.

CASS. We don't much.

LIZ. How much?

CASS. I don't know. It was one day in study hall.

LIZ. You sit at the same table in study hall?

CASS. No, we just—

LIZ. Sit together and laugh and giggle and talk about people behind their backs. Yeah, just like best buddies.

CASS. Liz—

LIZ. That's nice, Cass. You made a new friend. Why didn't you tell me about your new friend?

CASS. She's not my friend. I think she was lonesome or something. She just showed me her ring and asked me if I wanted to try it on.

LIZ. How cute. You and Sherri Lee engaged.

CASS. Funny, Liz.

LIZ. There's you a date for the prom, Cass. Yeah. You and Sherri Lee can go lezzie.

CASS. Shut up.

LIZ. Your prom picture would be so cute. *(Singsong.)*
"Cass and Sherri Lee-ee,
Cass and Sherri Lee-ee."

CASS. Shut UP! *(Beat)* It's not funny. And I'm not a lezzie.

LIZ. I was just kidding.

CASS. Then say it.

LIZ. What?

CASS. That I'm not a...

LIZ. Okay. You're not a lezzie. I was just kidding, Cass.

CASS. Well.

(PAULA BURGESS enters, but the other GIRLS don't see her yet. PAULA is obviously drunk. She is dressed in a hideous gown of green chiffon, the sleeves of which are of an even more voluminous fabric, perhaps pleated. With arms outstretched, the gown resembles one that might have been worn by a flamboyant evangelist, such as Aimee Semple McPherson. PAULA, however resembles

nothing so much as a drunken butterfly. One of her high heels is over her hand like a mitten, the other still on her foot. She wears the same paper heart as SHERRI LEE, with the number "39" printed on it. Her hair at one time was piled on top of her head, but now a lot of it has come down in wispy strands around her face. On her left wrist she wears an ugly Timex watch.)

Liz. You take everything so serious.

Paula. *(grandly) Good evening, ladies.* What time is it?

Liz. Paula, what are you doing?

Cass. You're supposed to be out front. *(PAULA looks completely bewildered.)*

Liz. Is the contest over? Who won, Paula?

Paula. It's not over. I don't think.

Cass. Do you have a pass? Paula?

Paula. Yep. I got one. *(turning a complete circle, looking around)* Somewhere I got a pass.

Cass. What's *wrong* with her? Are you sick? Paula? What is it?

Liz. *(smiling)* She's drunk as shit.

Cass. What?

Liz. *(delighted)* She's drunk! You're drunk, Paula!

Paula. *(pleased with herself)* Yep, I am! *(Then, seriously:)* What time is it?

Liz. She's drunk!

Cass. Oh, God! Get her *out.* Paula, go outside! You can't come back here.

Paula. *(suddenly ill)* I gotta sit down.

Cass. No. You can't.

Liz. Cass, let her sit down.

CASS. NO! She'll *never* get *up!* *(As if talking to someone deaf.)* PAULA! YOU! HAVE! TO! GO! MRS. TAYLOR! WILL! KILL! US!* *(CASS puts her arm around Paula.)* You gotta get a pass, Paula.

PAULA. I got—I got one. *(She suddenly slumps across the table in front of the lockers. Make-up and whatever falls to the floor. A note is pinned to the back of PAULA's gown.)*

LIZ. *(laughing)* Damn! Look, Cass. Mrs. Taylor pinned it to her gown. *(LIZ bends to retrieve make-up from floor.)* What does it say?

CASS. *(reading)* *"Please excuse Paula. She is drunk."*

LIZ. *(Laughs.)* No shit!

CASS. *(shaking PAULA)* Paula. Paula! Wake up!

PAULA. *(raising her head)* What? What time is it? Is it over?

LIZ. Paula, why did Mrs. Taylor send you back here?

PAULA. *(Stands up.)* I'm drunk!

LIZ. No shit!

PAULA. *(seriously)* I am!

LIZ. I can't believe it! Paula Burgess drunk as hell!

CASS. She's gonna be in so much trouble.

PAULA. *(Bewildered, whispers:)* Who is? Who's in trouble?

LIZ. Paula. Why did she send you to us?

PAULA. I got sick. I threw up.

CASS. Where?

PAULA. *(waving her arms expansively)* Everywhere!

CASS. In front of everybody?

PAULA. Huh?

CASS. Were you out on the stage?

PAULA. Noooo.

CASS. *(relieved)* Oh, good. That would be so embarrassing. Throwing up in front of the judges.

PAULA. I didn't.

CASS. I bet you're in trouble.

LIZ. Paula. What did Mrs. Taylor say?

PAULA. *(crossing to bench and sitting)* To come back here.

CASS. I bet she was mad.

PAULA. *(stretching out face-up)* I don't care. She's just a teacher.

CASS. *(crossing and standing above her)* Yeah. But what about your mother?

PAULA. Huh? *(CASS bends, rests her hands on the bench on either side of PAULA's head, her face above PAULA's.)*

CASS. Your mother!

PAULA. *(reaching up to tweak CASS' nose)* Oh, I didn't throw up on *Momma.*

CASS. *(straightening)* Paula, what number are you?

LIZ. She's thirty-nine.

PAULA. *(raising her head to check her number)* I'm thirty-nine!

CASS. And have you been out yet?

PAULA. Out where?

CASS. *Out,* Paula. Out there.

PAULA. Yep, I was out there.

CASS. In evening wear?

PAULA. Huh?

CASS. Paula, what are you wearing?

PAULA. *(looking down, because she's not sure)* A gown?

CASS. Right. And you're number thirty-nine?

PAULA. I'm thirty-nine.

LIZ. What are you doing, Cass?

CASS. And have you been out to be judged in evening wear?

PAULA. Nope.

CASS. *(summing up)* Well, don't you think your mother might be waiting to see how that dress looks on you?

PAULA. *(lazily)* She's seen it before, silly.

CASS. But has she seen it *tonight?*

PAULA. *(Suddenly realizing, she raises up, terrified.)* Oh, God!

CASS. That's right, Paula! What's gonna happen when they skip your number and your mother's out there waiting?

PAULA. *(Panicked, she rises.)* What am I gonna do?

LIZ. Calm down, Paula.

PAULA. Mama'll just die! What'll they do! *They'll announce it!* They're gonna announce over the loudspeaker why I'm not in the contest anymore! They will! Oh, God!

CASS. *(CASS grabs a hairbrush as a mock-microphone and jumps atop the bench. As the announcer:)* Testing—one—two—three! Uh, excuse me, ladies and gentlemen, there seems to be a slight change in the line-up tonight. Contestant Number Thirty-nine, Miss Paula Burgess, will not, I repeat, WILL NOT appear in evening wear, due to the fact that she is ... *shit-faced drunk!* Please make a note of this in your programs. We apologize for the inconvenience, and especially for the embarrassment to Mrs. Burgess, Paula's mother, sitting *right there! (She points past PAULA. PAULA, with a stricken expression, turns quickly to look where CASS points.)* Yes, folks, she's the lady with the Brownie Instamatic all focused and ready to shoot. Her daugher's drunk as Cooter Brown—so drunk she won't be in church tomorrow, her usual front-row seat will be vacant. Sad, but true. And that's all she wrote for Contestant Number Thirty-nine,—Miss Paula Burgess—*teenage alcoholic.*

PAULA. Oh, God. A alcoholic.

LIZ. Cass, that's mean.

PAULA. I'm a alcoholic. I am. I've heard all the signs. Drinking alone. That's the main sign.

LIZ. You're not an alcoholic.

PAULA. Yes, I am.

LIZ. No, you're not.

PAULA. How do you *know?*

LIZ. How many times have you been drunk?

PAULA. Since when?

LIZ. Since you first started drinking.

PAULA. *(terrified)* I can't remember!

LIZ. *When* did you take your very first drink?

PAULA. Tonight!

CASS. That proves it! An *instant* alcoholic!

LIZ. You're an instant bitch! You're just trying to get her upset.

CASS. I am not.

LIZ. She's messed up enough. Leave her alone.

CASS. I thought it might help sober her up. She doesn't know what's going on. She doesn't even know what time it is.

PAULA. *(snapping to, checking her watch)* Yessir, I do! It's fifteen minutes after nine o'clock!

Cass. Oh, God.

Paula. P.M.!

Cass. Oh, *God*. Look at her.

Paula. *(whispering)* Who?

Cass. *You!* Look, she's wearing a watch!

Paula. *(a loud whisper:)* Who is?

Cass. You are! She's wearing a watch in a beauty contest!

Liz. Shut up, Cass.

Cass. *Nobody* wears a watch in a beauty contest. *Nobody*. What were you gonna do with that watch, Paula? Go out there in that evening gown and all that make-up and say—"Hi, my name's Paula Burgess and I represent the Library Club and it's now — *(CASS looks at an imaginary watch.)* —nine-fifteen and all's well!

Liz. Shut up, Cass.

Cass. She's wearing a watch. *God*.

Paula. *(completely out of the blue)* Hey. Do y'all think we're gonna get home in time to watch "Saturday Night Live?"

Cass. Paula. Nobody wears a watch in a beauty contest.

Paula. I didn't *know*. I've never been in this stupid thing before.

Cass. You're not in it now, either.

Paula. I was for a little while.

Liz. A cameo appearance by Paula Burgess.

Paula. I have a cameo—with a *watch* in it. I shoulda worn that instead of this damned Timex. *(She pounds the watch with a shoe.)*

Cass. Timex? Yuck!

PAULA. I didn't *know!*

CASS. *Everybody* knows.

PAULA. How do *you* know? You've never been in this thing, either. *(eyeing CASS suspiciously)* What are you doing back here, anyway? *(Leans to Liz and whispers loudly:)* What is she doing back here, anyway?

LIZ. *(whispering loudly)* She's helping me.

PAULA. Oh. *(Looks down.)* Ooooh! I got something on my gown! I think I sat down in something. Mama told me not to sit down. *(Remembering Mama.)* Oh Lord—Mama. She's just gonna drop down dead.

LIZ. It'll probably come out.

PAULA. No, when they skip my number. Mama'll die.

LIZ. No, she won't.

PAULA. Yes, she will. She's talked about this thing for a month. She called every relative we've got and told them about it. All my aunts are out there. *(As PAULA's back is turned, CASS indicates with her arms how fat PAULA's aunts are.)*

LIZ. *(trying not to laugh)* Your mama's sisters?

PAULA. *(excitedly)* Yeah. Aunt JoAnn did my hair—she has a beauty shop in Jasper. *(LIZ and CASS suppress giggles.)* And Aunt Arnell did my make-up—she sells Avon.

CASS. Oh, Avon. *(She turns her face to LIZ.)* Yuck!

PAULA. *(spreading her arms to show off her dress)* And Aunt Christine made my dress.

LIZ. Really? It looks good. Doesn't it, Cass?

CASS. Yeah! *(to LIZ:)* I can't wait till it's finished.

PAULA. Huh?

LIZ. What did your Mama do?

PAULA. Nothing much. She's been so busy with Joanie and all.

LIZ. Paula's sister is pregnant.

CASS. I know. When's it due?

PAULA. Last week! She's big as a bull. She's here, too.

LIZ. Really?

PAULA. Yeah. They invite all the ones who've won it before. They get in free, I think.

CASS. I forgot—Joanie *was* Queen of Hearts.

PAULA. Yeah, the year before Daddy died.

LIZ. She was beautiful.

CASS. She still is. How old is she, anyway?

PAULA. Twenty-three.

CASS. *(amazed)* Twenty-three.

LIZ. She still looks good.

PAULA. Yeah. Anyway, they invite all the girls who're past Queen of Hearts. They call out their names and have 'em all stand up. *(She giggles.)*

CASS. What? *What?*

PAULA. *(giggling)* Joanie couldn't *get* up! I was watching through the curtains. She tried to, and Mama and them tried to help her up, but she just couldn't do it. She kinda—grunted—and rolled around on the bleachers.

CASS. She must be huge.

PAULA. Oh, she's all blowed up. After she'd groaned and wallered around and still couldn't get up, she just—waved at everybody.

CASS. God.

PAULA. You know, even though she's all bloated and everything, she's still pretty. She'll always be pretty.

Liz. Yeah. She's a natural beauty.

(SHERRI LEE Enters, waving a pass.)

Sherri Lee. Hey, y'all. I'm back.

Paula. Well, hey there, Sherri Lee! How's your hammer hanging?

Sherri Lee. *(not understanding)* What?

Paula. *(like a child)* Did you come to get me, Sherri Lee?

Sherri Lee. Not hardly, Paula. I don't think Mrs. Taylor wants to see you for a long, long time.

Paula. Why?

Sherri Lee. *(to Liz:)* You know what she did?

Paula. *(truly curious)* What?

Sherri Lee. *You* know. Don't play like you don't. That's why you're back here now and not out there with the rest of us.

Cass. *(saccharine)* Here's your earrings, Sherri Lee. Now why don't you just creep on back out front?

Sherri Lee. Do y'all know what she *did?*

Liz. She said she got sick.

Sherri Lee. *(delighted)* She vomited all over Mrs. Taylor!

Cass. Oh, God!

Paula. That's a lie! I only splashed on her shoes.

Cass. You *vomited* on Mrs. Taylor's shoes? Oh, God!

Paula. I couldn't help it.

Sherri Lee. Yes, you could. She did it on purpose.

Paula. It was a accident! She came over to me and stood right there in my face and her old perfume made me sick to my stomach.

LIZ. It *does* stink. What you reckon she wears?

PAULA. It's Ess-tee Louder and Ess-tee Louder *always* makes me sick to my stomach.

SHERRI LEE. There's not a thing wrong with Estée Lauder.

PAULA. Yeah, but Mrs. Taylor wears half a bottle and *drinks* the other half. It stinks. Anyway, she just stood there, right up in my face—so close I could see all the hairs up in her nose...

CASS. Gross!

PAULA. ...and she says, "Paula, have you been drinkin' a alcoholic beverage? Have you? You *have!* You have been drinkin' a alcoholic beverage" And that Ess-tee Louder smell was just a-rollin' offa her like heat-waves. So I tried to get around her, but she kept stepping in front of me. And then she grabbed me by my shoulders and started shaking me around. And I tried to tell her I was getting sick, 'cause I always get sick on the Ferris wheel and things like that, but she just kept on a-shakin' and a-stinkin' and a-shakin' and a-stinkin' and so, just to get her attention, I vomited on her shoes! *(PAULA makes a vomiting sound and bends down to SHERRI LEE's shoes. SHERRI LEE give a terrified shriek and rushes away.)*

CASS. Oh, God!

SHERRI LEE. It was a disgrace.

PAULA. *(Off-handedly.)* They were ugly shoes, anyway.

SHERRI LEE. Well, everybody knows about it. I wouldn't be a bit surprised if it's not in the newspaper Monday.

PAULA. You be sure and tell them about her Ess-tee Louder. *(Sniffs and looks nauseated.)*
Oh, I can still smell it! (Gags and spreads her cape.) I think the

fumes got on me! *(PAULA makes a beeline for the blowdryer on the dresser. She sits and turns the dryer on, blowing it directly into her face. Her hair billows wildly.)*

LIZ. *(Jumping away as PAULA heads for the dresser.)* Are you gonna be sick again?

PAULA. *(Her face tilted up into the dryer, eyes closed, taking deep breaths.)* No. No. I thought I was, but I'm not. I LOVE AIR! I JUST LOVE AIR! I believe I'll just sit here and think about something nice.

SHERRI LEE. Think how embarrassed your poor Mama's gonna be. *(Then, with mock pity.)* Oh, and what about your dead Daddy? *(PAULA switches the dryer off and tilts her head over so she can see SHERRI LEE. She takes a beat, then off handedly.)*

PAULA. He won't say anything.

SHERRI LEE. Well, it's a blessing he's dead and in the ground.

CASS. Here's your earrings, Sherri Lee. Now get out.

SHERRI LEE. *(Takes earrings and turns.)* Well, thank you, Cassie. I gotta go anyway. My number's coming up.

LIZ. You better believe it.

SHERRI LEE. *(smiling)* What?

LIZ. *(with snide enthusiasm)* Go out there and make us proud of you, Sherri Lee.

SHERRI LEE. Are you making fun of me, Liz?

LIZ. Me?

SHERRI LEE. Don't think you're fooling me, Liz Nichols. I know exactly how you feel about me.

LIZ. *(crossing away from her)* If you did, you wouldn't be here now.

SHERRI LEE. You're just jealous. It's like Mama says, all of y'all are just jealous of me. And I really can't blame you. Some people are just unattractive individuals.

CASS. Get your ugly ass outta here, Sherri Lee.

SHERRI LEE. *(sweetly)* Now, Cassie, I've never had any trouble with you. *(Crossing down to dressing table where PAULA is sitting. PAULA has been experimenting with make-up and is now studying a tube of bright red lipstick.)* You're a real sweet girl—when you're not with Liz. Everybody says so. *(SHERRI LEE bends to check her earrings.)* Everybody says you'd be a right nice girl if you weren't always trying to impress Liz.

PAULA. *(with the lipstick)* I love this shade. I just *love* this shade. Look, Sherri Lee, don't you just love — *(PAULA extends the lipstick, without looking, and it connects perfectly with SHERRI LEE's face, leaving a brilliant red slash.)*

SHERRI LEE. *(Screams and runs to mirror.)* OH! YOU DID THAT ON PURPOSE! You've ruined my make-up. You did that just so I wouldn't win!

PAULA. *(oblivious)* Win what?

SHERRI LEE. I always took you for you, too, when people said things about you. And now you do this! Well, I'm telling Mrs. Taylor! *(Exits.)*

LIZ and CASS. *(dancing around)* I'm gonna tell Mrs. Taylor! *(They laugh.)*

PAULA. What things? What things is she talking about, Liz?

LIZ. *(crossing to other dressing table)* I don't know, Paula.

PAULA. *(rising)* Cass? What things have they said? Sherri Lee—

LIZ. Sherri Lee makes things up.

PAULA. *(crossing to them)* No. Sherri Lee always tells the truth. What things did she mean?

CASS. Paula. I promise you...I *swear* to you...I have never heard anybody say anything about you that—I haven't said myself. *(CASS realizes this didn't come out exactly as she meant it. LIZ looks at her. CASS shrugs.)*

PAULA. *(somehow comforted)* Really?

CASS. Really.

PAULA. Okay. *(Crosses to bench opposite CASS and sits.)* Where's my purse? Do y'all see my purse?

CASS. *(rising and looking around)* No.

PAULA. *(pointing to several purses below table in front of lockers)* There it is, right there. *(CASS crosses to the purses.)* Right there by that ugly one.

CASS. *(Holds up a purse.)* By this ugly one?

PAULA. No, that one's mine.

CASS. *(Giggles and gives purse to PAULA.)* Oh.

PAULA. Thanks. *(Digging around inside purse, then she looks at the girls.)* I hate school. Don't y'all? Well, Liz, you probably like it. I mean, you're editor of the paper and head cheerleader and all. I guess that's fun.

LIZ. Not really.

PAULA. What? Editor or cheerleader?

LIZ. *(shrugging)* Newspaper's fun. But that cheerleader crap's pretty stupid.

CASS. It is not! It's a honor. And you've won awards and everything. It's a honor. Just like that out there.

PAULA. Out where?

LIZ. She means that shitty contest out there. *(Beat)* Oh. Sorry, Paula.

PAULA. I don't care. I didn't wanna be in it. Mama *made* me be in it.

CASS. Why?

PAULA. Oh, because Joanie was in it and won and everything. That's all I hear. "Joanie was Queen of Hearts. Joanie was on the Honor Roll." Joanie did this—Joanie did that. "Why can't you be like Joanie?" If I ever come up pregnant, all I have to say is, "But Mama—" *(PAULA pulls a bottle of gin from her purse and waves it around.)* —"Joanie did it, too!" *(She laughs and drinks from the bottle.)*

CASS. Oh, God! She's got alcohol back here! Mrs. Taylor's gonna kill us all!

LIZ. *(giggling)* Mrs. Taylor won't know.

CASS. What if she comes back here?

PAULA. She won't. She's in the restroom—soaking her shoes in the sink. Just sitting on the commode—crying.

LIZ. Here. Let me have some. *(Takes bottle and drinks.)* Hey, Cass. *(Holds out bottle.)* Taste it.

CASS. I don't want any.

LIZ. Just one taste.

CASS. Uh uh.

LIZ. Just one *taste. (She extends bottle. CASS sniffs it.)*

CASS. It smells like Pinesol.

LIZ. Taste it.

CASS. It's too strong.

LIZ. Okay. Chase it.

CASS. Huh?

LIZ. *(Gets a can of Coke.)* Chase it. Take a swig of gin, and then a swig of Coke—quick, though.

CASS. *(suspiciously)* Are you supposed to drink gin and Coke?

LIZ. Yeah, everybody does. Don't they, Paula?

PAULA. I just like mine plain.

LIZ. Try it.

CASS. Well. *(She takes a mouthful of gin and gags.)* Oh! *Shit!* *(Grabs the Coke can and drinks.)*

PAULA. Isn't it good?

CASS. *(smiling and pretending she likes it)* Pretty good! *(LIZ laughs, then CASS does, too.)*

PAULA. *(suddenly)* I hate my sister's guts.

CASS. What? *(still laughing)* You what?

PAULA. I hate Joanie's guts. I really hate her guts.

LIZ. Why?

PAULA. I always have. She thinks she's so perfect. Mama thinks so, too. Mama thinks Joanie never did a single bad thing in her whole life.

CASS. Well. Did she?

PAULA. No. *(LIZ and CASS laugh.)* Do y'all know she's read the whole Bible? Even the Table of Contents and the dictionary at the end.

LIZ. You're kidding.

PAULA. And when we were little and people would ask her what she wanted to be when she grew up, she'd say "A nun." Till she found out Baptist Churches don't *have* nuns.

CASS. God.

PAULA. She's always been that way. I reckon it's because she was born on Christmas.

CASS. Huh?

PAULA. Joanie says since she was born on Christmas,

she's always felt especially close to Jesus. *(LIZ and CASS giggle.)* Until she was thirteen years old, Mama always had to put *two* candles on Joanie's birthday cake. And Joanie would put the candles right up close together and light 'em and we'd all sing. *(She sings "Happy Birthday To You." to "Joanie and Jesus.")* And then, she'd just sit there—and watch the candles burn, until they burned all the way down and there was wax all over the top of the cake. Until the candles finally—went out.

LIZ. *(rapt)* And then what?

PAULA. She's *eat* it! The whole cake! That cow ate the whole cake while we just sat there and watched.

CASS. God.

PAULA. She's always been that way—*so holy.* She'd read books about all the saints and everything. About how they'd suffer and the real good ones would get the stigmata—you know, where they'd bleed from their hands or feet or somehwere. Joanie'd read those books about the saints and stay in her bedroom and light candles. Until one night, when she was twelve or thirteen, she came flying out of her bedroom, screaming that *she* had the stigmata—but it was just her period. *(LIZ and CASS howl.)* She was real disappointed.

LIZ. I bet she was.

PAULA. She tried. She's still trying. Married to a Baptist preacher. Pregnant as a pig. When what baby's born, y'all better look up in the sky, 'cause there's gonna be a Star in the East! *(She passes the bottle to CASS.)*

*Cautionary Note: Permission to produce this play does *not* include the rights to use this song. For rights, contact: Birch Tree Group Ltd., 180 Alexander Street, Princeton, NJ 08540

CASS. You know, the more you drink, the better it tastes.

LIZ. An instant alcoholic! That's what you are, Cass.

CASS. I bet I am. *(Takes another drink.)* This is good.

PAULA. I'm not going out there.

LIZ. When?

PAULA. When it's over. Mama'll be squalling and Joanie'll be preaching at me. I'm just not going.

CASS. You can't stay here all night.

PAULA. Yes, I can.

CASS. Somebody'd find you. The janitor'd find you.

PAULA. Mr. Leonard? He likes me. He's a nice man — *(then adding:)* — and a good janitor, too.

CASS. Uh uh. You better stay away from him. *(confidentially)* Y'all, they say that he's a sexual pervert person. Uh huh. He likes to touch a girl *down there.*

PAULA. *(whispering.)* Down *where?*

CASS. God, Paula. You just *cannot* be as dumb as you pretend.

PAULA. I'm not pretending. Am I, Liz?

LIZ. I'm afraid not, Paula.

PAULA. I know. *(rushing to lockers)* I'll hide in one of these lockers here.

LIZ. Forever?

PAULA. Yeah.

CASS. You'll miss the prom!

PAULA. I don't care.

CASS. And graduation. You'll miss graduation.

PAULA. I don't care about graduation, either.

LIZ. Aren't you going to college?

PAULA. *(forgetting her plans to hide)* Yeah. Walker College first—then the University.

Liz. Me too. What you gonna be?

Paula. *(becoming excited)* A physical therapist. That's all I've ever wanted to be.

Liz. Really?

Paula. Yep, all my life.

Liz. That's great, Paula.

Cass. Yuck. You don't wanna be a physical therapist.

Paula. *(warily)* Why not?

Cass. 'Cause you have to mess with all kinds of weird people and lots of 'em like to slobber and drool all over you and stuff. Uh uh, you do *not* wanna be a physical therapist.

Paula. Well, y'all — *(quickly)* —what *else* can I be?

Liz. How about a teacher? You might could teach science.

Cass. Or biology, like Mrs. Miller.

Liz. *(giggling)* Y'all remember Mrs. Miller in Biology? We got new books and they had a chapter about *sex!*

Cass. She was so mad, she stapled the whole chapter together. *(The GIRLS laugh.)*

Paula. I took my staples out.

Liz. So did I!

Cass. *(This never occurred to her.)* I didn't.

Liz. That's probably why you don't have a date for the prom, Cass.

Cass. LIZ!

Paula. Ohhhh. How *pitiful!*

Cass. I don't want a date.

Paula. *(cooing)* Ohhhh. That's the pitifullest thing I

ever heard in my whole life!

CASS. *(stomping off through stage left doorway)* Great! Now *everybody'll* know I'm the only girl in the whole senior class that doesn't have a date!

PAULA. Hey Cassie?

CASS. *(from offstage)* What?

PAULA. *(generously)* You can have mine.

CASS. *(still offstage)* Oh. *God!*

LIZ. What were you gonna do, Cass, keep it a secret?

CASS. *(still offstage)* Well—no.

LIZ. *(craftily)* I did.

PAULA. What?

LIZ. One time I didn't have a date and nobody ever knew.

CASS. *(intrigued, re-Entering)* That's crazy.

LIZ. It was our Valentine Banquet down at the church. I was thirteen years old and *could not* get a date to save my life.

PAULA. So you stayed at home and bawled and bawled until your mother told you to hush up and slapped your jaws, right?

LIZ. No, I went.

PAULA. But everybody felt sorry for you and all the other girls made their dates dance with you, right?

CASS. You can't dance at a *church* party, Paula.

PAULA. *(shrugging)* I can't dance, anyway.

LIZ. I went and nobody ever knew.

CASS. How?

LIZ. I got a jacket from my brother, see, and I took it down to the church an hour early and I put the jacket over the back of the chair next to mine and then I sat down to wait for the other kids. When they got there, I said my date, who was from *out-of-town,* was sorta sick and was in the bathroom.

CASS. I can't believe this.

LIZ. It's true! And I'd get up — *(She rises and crosses to doorway leading to gym.)* –and go to the bathroom door and say — *(She knocks on the wall.)* —"Kevin? Are you okay?" *(Beat)*

PAULA. And what did *he* say? *(LIZ and CASS exchange looks of disbelief.)*

LIZ. *(continuing)* I'd say "Can you come out? No? Well, hurry." And I'd go back and talk to my friends.

CASS. You did this all night?

LIZ. No. After a while, I told everybody we had to leave—that Kevin had messed up his shirt and I had to drive him home. And the door to outside was right by the bathroom, so I just pushed the door open and ran outside and nobody ever knew.

CASS. That's great. You're pretty smart, Liz.

PAULA. If she was smart, she'd a had a date.

LIZ. *(Laughs.)* Well, Paula, you've got some spunk after all.

PAULA. I got spunk. Yeah, I got spunk.

CASS. You're gonna need "spunk" when your mother gets a-hold of you.

PAULA. Oh, Lord. Mama.

CASS. *(echoing SHERRI LEE.)* And your dead daddy.

LIZ. Leave her alone.

CASS. I'm not hurting her.

LIZ. You love to start trouble, Cass. You love it.

CASS. *(still smiling but not understanding)* Why are you taking up for her? Why do you always side against me, Liz?

LIZ. *(putting her arm on PAULA's shoulder)* 'Cause I like her.

PAULA. Well, thank you!

CASS. *(grudgingly)* Well, I don't *not* like her.

PAULA. Well, thank *you.* *(Beat)* I think. *(crossing good-naturedly to CASS)* Oh, Cassie, I know you don't mean it. You're just upset because you can't find anybody who'll take you to the prom.

CASS. *(irritated)* Paula, for your information, I *have* a date to the prom.

PAULA. Who, Cass?

LIZ. *(amused)* Yeah. Who, Cass?

CASS. *(looking at her shoes)* I'm going with Eddie Akers.

LIZ. *(smiling)* Imagine that. I *never* woulda guessed. *What* a surprise!

CASS. *(firmly, to LIZ)* I'm *going* with Eddie Akers. *(Beat)*

PAULA. He's *odd.*

CASS. *(defensive)* He is not. He's a sweet boy. He drew my picture.

PAULA. I sit behind him in English. I used to think he was taking fantastic notes, 'cause he never stops writing. The whole class he writes like a mad-dog.

CASS. So?

PAULA. He goes to my church and, well, he's got problems. He can't decide whether to be a Jesus freak or a hell-raiser.

CASS. He's just a little confused.

PAULA. More than a little. One week, he'll rededicate his life to Jesus and next thing you know, he's out stealing road signs. Then he'll come back to church and walk the aisle and confess everything. Y'all, Eddie Akers has walked that aisle so many times, the deacons had to buy a new runner.

CASS. He's just mixed up.

PAULA. He's finally *cracked* up. I looked over his shoulder in English class to see what it was he was writing. It said "I Love Jesus, Damn It! Damn It! Damn It! *(She giggles.)* "I Love Jesus, Damn It! Damn It! Damn It!

(Off-stage, someone has started singing the "Queen of Hearts" theme.)

CASS. Well, I like him and he's taking me to the prom.

PAULA. I admit, he's got a nice voice. He sounds pretty good, y'all.

CASS. *(suddenly)* He's singing. *(They all listen.)* He *is!* He's singing!

LIZ. It's over. Queen of Hearts is over.

CASS. It can't be over yet. *(She starts out.)* Nobody's come back *in,* yet. *(She Exits to gym.)*

PAULA. I gotta hide. *(pacing frantically)* Liz, you gotta help me hide!

LIZ. *(hiding the gin bottle)* Paula, there's no place in here. Go hide in the restroom.

PAULA. I can't. Mrs. Taylor might still be in there crying. *(She smiles.)* You know, I think I'll send her a nice card or something — *(earnestly)* —just so she'll know I didn't mean to ruin her shoes. *(This thought appeals to her.)* Yeah. I will. I'll buy her a card—or a tasteful gift.

LIZ. *(smiling)* How about a new brand of perfume?

PAULA. *(agreeably)* That would be nice. *(explaining)* I just want her to know it was nothing personal, you know?

LIZ. Yeah.

PAULA. *(seriously)* I mean, when you vomit on somebody's shoes, you gotta be sure they don't misunderstand.

LIZ. I know what you mean.

(CASS runs back in, breathless.)

CASS. It's the worse thing that ever happened to Winston County High School. *(suddenly inspired)* Maybe even all of Double Springs.

PAULA. *(excited)* What?

LIZ. What, Cass?

CASS. *(gravely)* Sherri Lee won. She won, y'all.

LIZ. I was afraid of that. *(She sits.)* Damn.

PAULA. Sherri Lee won and I got kicked out. *(brighter)* Oh well, no use being depressed, y'all. I'll do better *next* year.

CASS. Paula, you *graduate* in *May.* Besides, your mama's gonna put you in reform school.

PAULA. *(horrified)* NO!

CASS. *(laughing)* Yeah, Paula. *Reform school!*

PAULA. *(near hysteria, running around)* Hide me! Y'all

help me hide!

(We hear APPLAUSE offstage.)

PAULA. They're all coming! They're coming back in here. They'll see me and tell Mama where I am! *(PAULA at center stage now.)* LIZ! CASS!

LIZ. *What,* Paula?

PAULA. *(suddenly pensive)* Do you reckon they have beauty contests in reform school? *(LIZ and CASS "swivel heads" and exchange a look, then:)*

BLACKOUT

ACT TWO

SCENE: The same. Some of the debris has been cleared. SHERRI LEE's overnight case remains, also her extra gown. A lot of the mess is still around, but the other contestants' personal belongings have been cleared from the stage.

TIME: One hour later.

AT RISE: CASS is alone onstage, sitting at the stage left dressing table, looking in the mirror, brushing her hair. The bottle of gin is on the table and CASS takes a drink, then resumes with her hair. The girls have ingested more of the liquor and this should be evident in their demeanor. Also, when CASS hears LIZ call Mrs. Taylor's name, She snatches up the bottle as if to hide it somehow. When it's apparent that Mrs. Taylor isn't coming into the dressing room, CASS relaxes.

Liz. *(offstage)* I will...Okay...See you Monday. *(Comes into view, then suddenly:)* Oh! *(She runs offstage again.)* The keys! Mrs. Taylor. You forgot to give me the keys! Thanks. Yeah, I will. Bye. *(Enters again.)*

Cass. You got the keys?

Liz. *(twirling keys on her finger)* I got the keys.

Cass. You got the keys!

Liz. I got the keys! *(Looks around.)* Hey. Is she still hiding, or what?

50

CASS. She's pouting.

LIZ. *(as if addressing a child:)* Paula? Are you pouting?

CASS. She might be passed out.

LIZ. Hell, we drank as much as she did.

PAULA. *(Her head pops up over the side of the refrigerator crate.)* You did not! *(She drops back into the crate.)*

LIZ. Paula, me and Cass drank a lot more than you did. You didn't drink hardly any. Paula?

PAULA. *(from inside crate)* I think I'm hyperventilating.

CASS. She's what? What did she say?

PAULA. *(still inside box)* I can't breathe, damn it. I'm gonna be sick.

CASS. Breathe deep, Paula.

PAULA. I *am*—I'm hyperventilating.

CASS. What does that *mean?*

PAULA. It stinks in here.

LIZ. Did you get sick again?

PAULA. No, but I almost did. It stinks in here.

CASS. What does it smell like?

PAULA. There's mothballs in here.

LIZ. *(giggling)* I didn't know moths had balls.

CASS. *(taking up the joke)* I bet they do!

PAULA. I bet the big ones do. Them big ones. What're they called?

CASS. The big green ones? Like in biology?

LIZ. Luna moths.

PAULA. I always called them helicopter bugs. *(Her head pops up over the top of the crate.)* That's what they look like to me. Helicopter bugs.

LIZ. I guess they do.

PAULA. I remember one time, at a revival our church was having, Mama made me go because Joanie was singing a solo for the special music. Boy, she thought she was something, too. Standing up there singing. She'd memorized all the words so she could concentrate on the emotion. She was up there just bellerin'—singing "Reach Out To Jesus"— y'all know that one? *(The GIRLS nod.)* She was singing "Reach Out To Jesus" and I looked up at the ceiling—and that's when I saw it. It was just about the biggest helicopter bug I'd ever seen.

CASS. Luna moth.

PAULA. Yeah. And it was sailing along up close to the ceiling—up around the lights. And Joanie was singing: *(PAULA sings and waves her hands, conducting.)*
"He is always there,
Hearing every prayer,
Faithful and true."

And that helicopter bug—

CASS. Luna moth.

PAULA. —he was just a-sailing along, just waiting. And Joanie was really getting all worked up, singing: *(PAULA sings and conducts again. This time the other two GIRLS sing along.)*
"Walking by His side,
In His love we hide,
All the day through."
(PAULA "cuts them off" with her conducting.) And everybody in the whole church was glued to Joanie—she had 'em all to where they couldn't hardly wait for her big finish. And

I was watching that helicopter—and all of a sudden—I *prayed*. I prayed so hard, I was scared I'd prayed it out loud. I didn't, but it seemed like it. I prayed: "Dear God, if You are really real—if You're really there, just do one thing for me and I'll never ask You for another thing as long as I live—*so help me God!* Dear God— *(Beat)* Make that helicopter bug *attack!*"

CASS. Did He?

PAULA. And Joanie's big part was coming. I'd seen her practice it in the mirror a hundred times. She had it down pat, too. She had this little *catch* in her voice, kinda like a mix between Linda Ronstadt and Ethel Waters—and she'd throw her head back and kinda flutter her eyelids and look real pitiful, like—*Jesse* on "General Hospital." And it worked! She had them people about ready to walk the aisle and there hadn't even been any preaching yet. And I was praying as hard as I could— *(hands clasped)* "Attack, God! *Attack!* And Joanie knew she was doing good. And then, she sang her *favorite part: (singing:)*
"When you get discouraged
Just remember what to do.
(PAULA extends her arms heavenward.)
"Reach out to Jesussss..."
(She brings one hand down to her mouth rapidly and dives back into the crate. LIZ and CASS are laughing wildly. Then one of PAULA'S hands curls over the top of the crate. LIZ points and She and CASS laugh even more as the other hand appears. Finally, PAULA'S head and shoulders appear.) And I tell you, I *know* there is a God and He heard my prayer. *(LIZ and CASS howl.)* You may think that helicopter bug was attracted to Joanie's eyelashes fluttering around—but I *know.* I

know that God answers prayers. That bug swooped down like a Japanese dive bomber and flew straight into Joanie's mouth and it like to choked her to death before the preacher could run his hand down her throat and pull it out. He throwed it down on the floor and stepped on it.

CASS. God.

PAULA. Joanie was so hysterical—she never did get over it. And you know what else? When everybody in her biology class was doing insect collections, Mrs. Miller let Joanie collect leaves instead. Bugs made her break out.

LIZ. *(still laughing)* Oh. That's great.

PAULA. *(remembering)* The preacher, he stomped that moth to death. After church was over and everybody had gone downstairs to the fellowship hall, I went back and picked that moth up offa the floor and put it in my pocket and took it home.

CASS. You're kidding.

PAULA. Nope. I put it in my Bible. I look at it all the time. It's pretty. *(seriously)* I wouldn't take nothing for it, neither. *(Two beats)*

LIZ. Hey, Paula. What's in there?

PAULA. Where?

LIZ. In that box.

PAULA. Old band uniforms.

CASS. How old?

PAULA. *(ducking back down into the crate)* *Real* old.

LIZ. Older than us?

PAULA. *(still in crate)* I think. I don't remember seeing the band wearing anything like these.

CASS. They used to wear plumes.

PAULA. *(unable to hear)* What?

LIZ. *(loudly, to the crate:)* Plumes! Cass said the band used to wear plumes.

PAULA. Did you?

LIZ. I'm not in the band, Paula. I'm a cheerleader.

PAULA. Same thing.

CASS. It is not. Cheerleader is better. Cheerleaders get to stay out the whole game. Band's only on the football field ten minutes.

PAULA. Oh.

CASS. Anyway, they used to wear plumes.

PAULA. Like feathers!

CASS. Yeah. My brother did.

PAULA. Huh?

LIZ. *(loudly)* She said "Yeah." When her brother was in the band.

CASS. One time, when we played Addison, the band did a lights-out show.

PAULA. What?

LIZ and CASS. *(screaming at the crate)* A LIGHTS-OUT SHOW! *(LIZ and CASS look at each other and laugh.)*

LIZ. The band did a lights-out show!

PAULA. Really?

CASS. Yeah.

PAULA. What's that?

CASS. During half-time, they turned all the lights out.

PAULA. *(still in box)* I don't get it.

(CASS switches the overhead LIGHTS "OFF.")

CASS. They turned out all the football lights and everybody in the band had these little flashlights tied to their plumes. *(She jumps atop one of the benches.)*

PAULA. Flashlights?

CASS. *(motioning for LIZ to join her on the other bench)* Yeah. And when all the lights went out, they turned on their little flashlights— *(CASS pantomimes this and says:)* Bink!

LIZ. *(copying her, giggling)* Bink!

CASS. And they all got in a straight line and played "Glow Worm."

PAULA. What?

LIZ and CASS. *(screaming again)* THEY PLAYED "GLOW WORM."

CASS. *(singing "Glow Worm"* and marching down the bench, joined at the second line by LIZ)* *(Beat)*

PAULA. *(from the crate)* Oh. How *pitiful.*

CASS. No. It was real impressive.

(She switches the overhead LIGHTS back "ON.")

LIZ. *(creeping up the bench)* Paula? Come out of there.

PAULA. No, I like it.

LIZ. Just about everybody's gone.

PAULA. Who?

LIZ. Everybody but Mrs. Robins. She's counting the money. *(striking a pose)* And Sherri Lee's posing for pictures. *(CASS makes clicking noises, as if photographing LIZ.)*

---

*Cautionary Note: Although the tune of this song is Public Domain in the U.S. the English lyrics by Johnny Mercer & Lilla Cayley Robinson are not. Rights to use these lyrics in production must be procured from: Marks Music Co., c/o Hudson Bay Music, Inc., 1619 Broadway, New York, NY 10019.

PAULA. Mrs. Taylor's gone?

LIZ. She gave me the keys to lock up.

PAULA. Why?

LIZ. Because I'm *supposed* to lock up.

PAULA. What about my mother?

LIZ. I didn't see her.

PAULA. I'm coming out!

CASS. We don't care. Stay in there forever.

PAULA. *(sing-song)* I've got a surprise for you.

LIZ. *(sing-song)* What is it, Paula?

PAULA. *(sing-song)* I'm not in "Queen of Hearts" any-more. *(LIZ and CASS exchange glances.)*

LIZ and CASS. No shit!

PAULA. I've changed, ya'll. *(LIZ and CASS tip the crate forward.)*

LIZ. Come on out, Paula. *(They look inside the crate, then laugh. PAULA slowly crawls out on all fours, onto the floor and up onto the bench, inching down it. She is wearing a sequined majorette uniform, a huge band member's hat, and majorette ankle-boots.)*

CASS. God. *(PAULA sings the first four lines of "Glow Worm."* when she reaches the downstage end of the bench, she raises up on her knees, spreading her arms wide.)* Well, here I am! *(Beat) Applaud! (LIZ and CASS applaud. PAULA stands on the bench.)* I'm the "Pride of Winston County."

LIZ. I'm proud.

CASS. I am, too.

PAULA. Yeah, I'm Sherri Lee Speer and I can twirl any-thing twirlable.

*See Note, p. 56.

LIZ. Can you twirl a baton?

PAULA. Like you've never seen.

CASS. Can you twirl fire?

PAULA. You bet your ass I can. *(CASS retrieves a baton that spilled from the crate.)*

CASS. *(giving the baton to PAULA)* Well, here you go, Sherri Lee. *(PAULA begins twirling, quite awkwardly, and stomping around on the bench.)*

PAULA.
"I'm from Winston,
Couldn't be prouder.
If you don't believe me,
I'll yell a little louder!"
(She drops the baton and picks it up. LIZ and CASS applaud.)

CASS. You'd be a *good* feature twirler.

PAULA. Oh, I know it. I'm Sherri Lee Speer and I'm beautiful and I'm talented and I want you all to know that, whatever I am, I owe it to the Lord.

CASS. Amen.

PAULA. *(twirling and singing to the tune of "Stand Up for Jesus")*
"I twirl, I twirl for Jesus,
And for the Good Lord, too."

LIZ. Paula!

PAULA. And I don't never smoke. And I don't never drink. And I only let boys kiss me on the hand and cheek, because my body is sacred. My body is a temple.

LIZ. "Sherri-Lee Temple!"

PAULA. Yeah! *(She sings the first two lines of "On the Good*

Ship Lollipop," *substituting the word "bed" in the 2nd line, then claps her hand over her mouth, feigning shock.)* Oh no! Did I say "bed"? No, I meant to say "twin beds." *(They all laugh.)*

CASS. *(picking up pom-pons)*
"Two, four, six, eight!
Who do we appreciate?
Paula, Pau—"

PAULA. *(suddenly serious)* "SHERRI LEE! Sherri Lee.

CASS. *(with no enthusiasm)* Sherri Lee. Sherri Lee. Yea.

PAULA. *(still twirling)* You know— *(She drops the baton.)* Oh. Do do!

CASS. She said "do do!" Sherri Lee said "do do!"

PAULA. Noooo, I'm Paula now.

CASS. Ohhh.

PAULA. *(Picks up baton and twirls again.)* You know, when I was little, just real little, we were—

LIZ. *(interrogating)* Who's we?

PAULA. We! My family and me.

LIZ. Ohhh.

PAULA. *(resuming her story)* Anyway, we were in Fort Lauderdale and it was back when I was little—just real little.

CASS. *(face to face with PAULA)* How little?

PAULA. *(looking down and tapping Cass' breasts with her baton)* About as little as your titties! *(LIZ laughs loudly. CASS covers her breasts with her arms and crosses to LIZ.)*

CASS. Shut up! *(LIZ tries to stop laughing.)*

PAULA. Anyway, I was real little. It was back during all

*Cautionary Note: Permission to produce this play does *not* include permission to use this song in production. For rights, contact: Whiting Music Corp., 836 Riomor Dr., Vero Beach, CA 32960

the racial stuff, you know? The marches and all? And I'd seen these people—white people—on television, marching and stuff. So there we are, driving down the street in Fort Lauderdale and I'm hanging out the window screaming:
"Two, four, six, eight—
I don't wanna integrate!"
    Cass. Oh, God!
    Paula. Yeah, and people started throwing seashells at our car. *(Points to eyelid.)* That's how I got this scar here. Mama like to slapped me baldheaded, too. And I didn't even know what "integrate" meant!

(NOISES of SHERRI LEE being congratulated off-stage.)

    Cass. *(regarding SHERRI LEE's impending entrance)* Do you know now?
    Paula. Yeah.

(More NOISE from off-stage. They all react.)

    Cass. Well that's good, because y'all, *we* are being *integrated!*

(CASS manages to stand and hide the bottle behind her back. Then SHERRI LEE Enters, looking off-stage, wearing a rhinestone tiara, a sash that reads "Queen of Hearts 1976" and holding a dozen roses and a large trophy in her arms.)

    Sherri Lee. *(speaking to someone offstage)* Thank you. Thank you.

(We see the FLASH of photos being taken. LIZ, CASS and PAULA mimic SHERRI LEE's posings.)

SHERRI LEE: I'm just thrilled to death. Oh, I could just die.

LIZ. We wish you would.

SHERRI LEE. *(to off-stage:)* Thank you. Could we do one more? Pretty please?

(Another FLASH. Then someone off-stage hands SHERRI LEE her Polaroid camera.)

SHERRI LEE. Thank you. Bye-Bye. Happy Easter! *(She turns to face the girls. LIZ drops dramatically to her knees, hands clasped in fervent prayer.)*

LIZ. *Attack, God! ATTACK! (Two beats)*

SHERRI LEE. *(trying to maintain her smile)* What?

LIZ. *(rising)* Oh, I was just praying. *(CASS and PAULA giggle. SHERRI LEE regards them. LIZ giggles. SHERRI LEE realizes the joke is on her and lifts her head. She crosses to dressing table to deposit trophy, roses, and camera. She pulls a photo from the camera and peels off the emulsion, pretending to study it while the other GIRLS try unsuccessfully to suppress their laughter.)*

SHERRI LEE. *(studying the Polaroid)* I smell alcohol. *(The other girls giggle. SHERRI LEE faces them.)* I can smell an alcoholic drink.

CASS. It's umm—just your imagination.

SHERRI LEE. No. No ma'am. I definitely smell alcohol.

PAULA. *(confidentially)* Well now, Sherri Lee, I know I can't fool *you (Beat)* —I've been drinking.

SHERRI LEE. Nope. I smell fresh alcohol. Have y'all got

alcohol in this room? Liz Nichols, do you have alcohol in here?

Cass. *(sniffing loudly)* Alcohol. Alcohol! I detect *alcohol.*

Sherri Lee. *(Disgusted, as the others laugh.)* Oh, Cass, please.

Paula. That crown sure is shiny, Sherri Lee.

Sherri Lee. Thank you, Paula. And how are you feeling?

Paula. Much better, thank you.

Cass. *(behind SHERRI LEE.)* Yeah, she took some medicine and now she's feeling all better.

Sherri Lee. Oh? What kind of medicine? A Alka-Seltzer?

Paula. *(giggling, as CASS waves the bottle, unseen by SHERRI LEE.)* Nooo.

Sherri Lee. What kind, then?

Paula. *(looking at LIZ and CASS, rolling her eyes)* I don't know.

Sherri Lee. Didn't it have a label on it? *(LIZ, CASS and PAULA all giggle at this, CASS still waving the bottle.)*

Paula. Yeah. Yeah, it had a label.

Sherri Lee. Then what kind of medicine—

Cass. *(waving bottle in her face)* This kind of medicine, Sherri Lee! See? This kind. *See? See?*

Sherri Lee. *(grabbing bottle from CASS)* Alcohol!

Paula. Yeah!

Sherri Lee. I knew it! I knew it!

Paula. *(grabbing bottle from SHERRI LEE and crossing away)* I love it! I love it! I love alcohol. Oh, *God* I love it! *(She lifts bottle.)* It's so wonderful. *(Takes a big drink, then:)* It's better than sex. *(Beat)*

Liz. *(laughing)* What did you say?

PAULA. I said alcohol is better than sex.

CASS. What do you know about sex?

PAULA. I know lots.

LIZ. When have you ever had sex?

PAULA. Lots of times. Lots and lots.

LIZ. You've had sex.

PAULA. Sure.

LIZ. Who with?

PAULA. *(thrown a bit)* Huh?

LIZ. You've had sex. So tell us, who with? *(Beat)*

PAULA. *(off-handedly)* Well, never with anybody *else*. *(LIZ howls.)*

CASS. Oh, *God!*

SHERRI LEE. I cannot believe my ears.

CASS. Now Sherri Lee's gonna have to go boil her ears out with peroxide.

SHERRI LEE. I am not.

CASS. What are you doing back here anyway?

SHERRI LEE. I'm just waiting for my ride.

CASS. The queen is waiting for her royal carriage.

LIZ. Cass.

CASS. *(raising SHERRI LEE's hand to see the diamond ring)* Where's your boyfriend, Sherri Lee? Where's the famous Mark Patterson we've all heard so much about?

SHERRI LEE. He had to work because of Easter tomorrow. He called me and said he'd try to get here in time.

CASS. To see you win. How adorable.

SHERRI LEE. *(irritated)* That's not what I meant, Cass.

PAULA. Where does he work?

SHERRI LEE. *(crossing in to PAULA.)* He lives in Mobile. He works for U.P.S.

PAULA. U.P.S. *(smiles)* He works for "Ups."

LIZ. *(doing Groucho)* It has its ups and downs.

SHERRI LEE. *(not amused)* That's funny, Liz. I'll have to tell Mark.

LIZ. Feel free.

SHERRI LEE. *(to PAULA.)* It's United Parcel Service. He drives a delivery truck.

PAULA. Oh.

CASS. Too bad he couldn't deliver himself to the Queen of Hearts contest tonight.

SHERRI LEE. He'll be here. And I'll just wait right here on him. *(trying her best to charm the three girls)* He sent me some candy. Want some? *(She opens a box of chocolates. Silence.)* Paula? Want some? *(PAULA takes the entire box.)*

CASS. From Mobile to here? That's a long drive, Sherri Lee.

SHERRI LEE. I'll wait.

PAULA. *(eating chocolate) (During the next several minutes, PAULA consumes quite a lot of the candy. This should be subtle and doesn't draw undue attention.)* Is *your* mother out there, too?

SHERRI LEE. No, she went home when it was over. She had to fix Corey's Easter basket.

PAULA. I hope Mama remembers to fix mine.

CASS. You still get a Easter basket?

PAULA. She fixes Joanie one, too. She always gives me tons of chocolate and stuff.

SHERRI LEE. I think that's cute.

CASS. *(to LIZ, mocking SHERRI LEE)* "Cute."

LIZ. So...Sherri Lee, tell us...how does it feel? *(Her voice has the tone of a TV commentator, perhaps Howard Cosell, as she circles the room.)* I mean, only two weeks ago, you barely got nominated into the competition. Yes, thanks to the Agriculture class, you made it in—just by the hair of your chinny chin chin. *(She is standing next to PAULA.)*

PAULA. *(extending liquor bottle, giggling)* Gin!

LIZ. *(taking bottle from Paula, drinking)* And now, look at you...you have succeeded in walking away with the "big one." *(using the bottle as a mock-microphone)* Yes folks, it's a Cinderella story come true. Share with us, if you will, Sherri Lee, your thoughts, your emotions, your deepdown heartfelt feelings on this night of nights. Miss Sherri Lee Speer—Queen of Hearts, Nineteen Seventy-Six...*How* does it feel? *(SHERRI LEE has been staring at LIZ, her anger building. She grabs the bottle that LIZ has extended toward her, as a mike.)*

SHERRI LEE. *(smiling)* Well, I'll tell you, Liz...it feels good. *(Takes a huge drink from the bottle.)* Yeah, it feels pretty fucking good. *(The other GIRLS sit in shock. Count four.)*

PAULA. Wha—um, *what* did she say?

CASS. Oh, *God!*

LIZ. I can't believe it.

PAULA. She said—you said the "F" word. She said the "F" word. Didn't you? Didn't she, y'all?

SHERRI LEE. Bet your ass, Paula.

PAULA. She said the "F" word. I've *never* heard anybody say it in person. Never.

SHERRI LEE. Want me to say it again?

PAULA. No. I don't like it.

LIZ. What's going on, Sherri Lee?

PAULA. I've never in my life even *thought* that word. *Ever.*

SHERRI LEE. Oh, I don't believe that.

PAULA. It's the truth. I'd never say the "F" word. Or G.D., either. G.D. is just as bad.

SHERRI LEE. Paula, you try too hard to be something you're not.

PAULA. No, I don't.

LIZ. Sherri Lee, what are you trying to pull?

SHERRI LEE. *(still to PAULA:)* You want everybody to like you, so you try to be exactly what everybody wants you to be.

PAULA. You're just saying that because nobody likes *you.*

SHERRI LEE. *(enjoying this)* Why, you're getting hostile, Paula.

PAULA. I am not.

SHERRI LEE. I believe you are.

PAULA. No. No, I'm not.

SHERRI LEE. Well, then, there's something else.

PAULA. What?

SHERRI LEE. If I tell you, you'll get mad.

PAULA. No, I won't.

LIZ. *(softly)* Cass, what's she trying to do?

SHERRI LEE. Promise?

PAULA. I promise.

SHERRI LEE. Okay. You wanna know your biggest fault?

PAULA. *(not so sure)* Yeah.

SHERRI LEE. And you won't get mad?

PAULA. I promise. What is it?

SHERRI LEE. Paula, you simply *cannot* take constructive criticism. *(Beat)*

PAULA. *(suddenly furious)* THAT'S A GODDAMNED LIE! *(SHERRI LEE laughs. PAULA is suddenly aware of what has happened. She puts her hands to her mouth.)* Oh, no! I said it. I said it, y'all. *(She is really upset.)* I think I'm gonna be sick!

CASS. *(going to her)* Paula, it's no big deal.

PAULA. Yes! Yes, it is, too.

CASS. *(trying to soothe her)* No, it's really not, Paula.

PAULA. Oh. God's gonna hate me, now. He's just gonna hate my guts. *(She puts her head in her hands.)*

LIZ. *(to SHERRI LEE:)* See what you did?

CASS. Paula, God is not gonna hate you. God doesn't do things like that.

PAULA. Oh, yes He *does.* God gets mad. God gets fed up. I mean, He's only human.

LIZ. Right, Paula.

PAULA. God's gonna just kill me.

SHERRI LEE. Paula? *(Her tone is comforting.)* I've always liked you, Paula. Ever since I came here, I liked you. *(PAULA doesn't look up. LIZ and CASS exchange puzzled glances.)* Yeah, I always have. And you know what else? Tonight, when we all voted on Miss Congeniality—I voted for you. *(PAULA raises her head.)* Yeah, I did. I voted for *you,* Paula.

PAULA. *(intrigued)* Really? *(She looks down at her majorette uniform, then flatly:)* Why?

SHERRI LEE. You're a good person, Paula.

PAULA. *(shaking her head)* No. No I'm not.

SHERRI LEE. *(soothing)* Yeah. Yeah, I could tell the first

time I ever saw you. The very first time. I could tell.

PAULA. *(timidly)* I remember when I saw you the first time.

SHERRI LEE. *(eagerly)* When?

LIZ. *(to CASS:)* I love reminiscing, don't you?

CASS. *Umm humm.*

PAULA. *(Goes to SHERRI LEE.)* I walked into class and you were up at the board. Somebody had drawn a picture of the brain—

SHERRI LEE. And I was labeling it!

CASS. *(to LIZ, mockingly:)* She was labeling it!

LIZ. *(deadpan)* Just imagine the stories they can tell their grandchildren.

PAULA. *(sitting near SHERRI LEE)* Yeah, you were writing out all the different parts. Like um, medulla oblongata, and um, the cerebellum...

SHERRI LEE. Yeah.

PAULA. And I asked whoever was sitting by me... *(remembering)* It was Diane Batson, and I said, "Diane. Who's that up there?" And Diane didn't even look up from her paper, she was labeling the brain, and she mumbled "Cere-bellum" — so I called you Sara for three weeks. *(They laugh.)*

SHERRI LEE. Oh, no! That's neat!

CASS. *Neat.*

SHERRI LEE. *(raising the bottle)* Well, here's to Miss Sara Bellum. *(She drinks, then passes it to PAULA.)*

CASS. I can't believe this.

PAULA. *(Delighted, passes bottle back to SHERRI LEE.)* You can have the rest.

SHERRI LEE. I don't really like gin. It's not my favorite, I mean. You know what's good? Tequila!

PAULA. Really?

CASS. *(crossing to them)* Sherri Lee, would you like to explain yourself?

SHERRI LEE. What do you mean?

CASS. Coming in here cussing and drinking.

SHERRI LEE. Well, I'll tell you, Cass. I'm cussing and drinking. *(She raises bottle and laughs. PAULA laughs too.)*

CASS. But why?

SHERRI LEE. Huh?

CASS. *(adamant)* Why?

SHERRI LEE. Why *what?*

LIZ. What happened to Little Miss Bible School?

SHERRI LEE. Oh. *(giggles)* Is that what y'all call me? Miss Bible School? *(Rises and holds bottle up.)* Well, girls— school's out! *(SHERRI LEE extends bottle to LIZ.)* Come on, Liz. Have a drink.

LIZ. *(ignoring SHERRI LEE's attempt to join in)* What are you trying to do, Sherri Lee? *(Beat, during which SHERRI LEE realizes she will not be allowed to join "the gang.")*

SHERRI LEE. Nothing. *(a bit forced)* Just have a little fun. Aren't y'all having fun? I am. Are you having fun, Paula?

PAULA. *(confused)* I don't know.

SHERRI LEE. Are you having fun, Liz?

LIZ. *(studying SHERRI LEE)* Yeah. Yeah, I'm having fun, Sherri Lee.

SHERRI LEE. Well, good. 'Cause if y'all aren't having fun, we can always play games.

PAULA. I'm not good at cards.

SHERRI LEE. *(regarding LIZ)* I didn't mean cards, Paula.

PAULA. *(continuing)* All I can play is Old Maid and Strip Poker—and I always get 'em mixed up.

LIZ. *(laughing)* Face it, Paula—that's the story of your life!

PAULA. *(taking the wrong way)* That was an ugly thing to say.

LIZ. Just kidding, Paula.

PAULA. It wasn't funny, it was hateful.

LIZ. *(meekly)* Okay.

SHERRI LEE. *(trying again)* Well y'all, what are we gonna do?

CASS. *(crossing to her)* "We?" Sherri Lee, you don't fit in. You can't say "we" because *you* are not *us.*

SHERRI LEE. How do you know that, Cass?

CASS. Well, because I—

SHERRI LEE. *(very angry)* Who do you think *you* are, Cass? Nobody. That's what you are—nothing but a shadow. Liz's shadow.

LIZ. *(a warning)* Don't start that, Sherri Lee.

SHERRI LEE. If it wasn't for Liz, nobody'd even see you. You know what "reflected glory" is, Cass? That's you. Living in reflected glory from Liz.

CASS. *(Her voice quavers.)* You can't say that to me. *(Beat)* Liz. It's not true. *(LIZ is looking down. CASS touches her.)* Tell her it's not true!

LIZ. *(with little conviction)* Well no ... it's not true, Cass. *(to SHERRI LEE)* It's not true. *(SHERRI LEE laughs.)*

SHERRI LEE. I'm not sure she convinced me. How about you, Paula? *(PAULA doesn't answer.)* How about *you,* Liz? Did you convince *yourself?* *(LIZ glares at SHERRI LEE.)*

CASS. *(looking from LIZ to SHERRI LEE, not really understanding) (She is near tears.)* Sherri Lee, you're up to something. I don't know what, because you won't tell us. Either that or you're a split personality or something.

SHERRI LEE. *(calmly)* Cass. You always try to figure everything and everybody out. But you don't *know* and you couldn't understand. You don't *know.*

LIZ. *(turning from SHERRI LEE)* That's right. We don't know. *(She crosses to CASS, who turns away, wiping tears.)*

PAULA. Don't know what?

LIZ. And we don't *want* to know.

PAULA. What, Sherri Lee?

SHERRI LEE. See, it's a game I play. I've been doing it a long time.

PAULA. Doing what?

SHERRI LEE. Being different people. I like to be different people.

CASS. She's crazy. You're crazy.

SHERRI LEE. No. But I *can* be crazy if you want me to.

PAULA. I think I'm lost.

SHERRI LEE. *(excitedly)* I can be anything. I... *(explaining)* I've never lived in one place more than two years— sometimes not even half a year. I don't know how many schools I've been in. Every time I'd start to get settled, Daddy'd get transferred.

CASS. Lots of people move around.

SHERRI LEE. Have you ever moved?

CASS. No.

SHERRI LEE. Then shut up, Cass. *(to PAULA:)* When I was in the ninth grade, I decided to do things a different way. I'd be somebody else. A completely different person—just to see what would happen. How other people would act to me. Every time I'd go to a new school, I'd be somebody else. And it's always somebody I knew from the *last* school.

CASS. That's stupid.

SHERRI LEE. No, it's true. *(excitedly)* See I was in Mobile before I came here. There was this girl down there— Tamara Thomas. And that's who I've been here. I've been Tamara Thomas. *(Laughs.)* She was a real snot and the biggest goody-goody ever. So I've been Tamara.

CASS. You're pretty stupid, Sherri Lee. Or is Sherri Lee a made-up name?

SHERRI LEE. *(annoyed)* It's my real name. And I am nowhere near stupid. When I was four, I took an I.Q. test. A hundred forty-six. Hundred forty's genius. So don't call me stupid, Cass. I'm not stupid.

CASS. *(disturbed)* Well, you're crazy then.

SHERRI LEE. *(trying to make her understand)* I just did it to see what would happen. Sorta a hobby. I didn't mean to upset anybody.

LIZ. *(incredulous)* You didn't mean to *upset* anybody?

CASS. *(shrugging)* Who's upset?

PAULA. *(raising her hand, as if in class)* I am.

SHERRI LEE. *(trying to continue her explanations)* Y'all, I didn't mean—

LIZ. *(deliberately silencing SHERRI LEE)* Why, Paula?

Why are you upset *now?*

PAULA. Mama's gonna squall about how I embarrassed her in front of the whole town. Then she'll start in about Daddy and how ashamed he'd be if he was living. I can't stand it when she talks about what Daddy would say and what Daddy would do. *(Beat)* I think I'll kill myself.

LIZ. Don't be silly, Paula.

PAULA. I will. I'll kill myself.

CASS. You will not kill yourself.

PAULA. Yes ma'am, I sure will!

CASS. She wants attention so bad she'd do anything for it.

PAULA. That's a lie, Cass.

CASS. You will *not* kill yourself, Paula.

PAULA. Yes, I will, too. I've done it lots of times.

SHERRI LEE. *(softly)* When?

PAULA. Once, when I was thirteen years-old. I was fat. I was real fat.

CASS. *(remembering)* "Paula the Piglet."

PAULA. Yeah. And I was real depressed.

SHERRI LEE. Why?

PAULA. Because I was fat and then all my fish died.

LIZ. Your fish?

PAULA. In my aquarium. They all died from some kind of fish disease. So I decided to kill myself.

SHERRI LEE. How?

PAULA. Well, I didn't have any drugs or poison, and I couldn't cut my wrists because blood makes me sick to my stomach. So I decided to hang myself.

Liz. Because your *fish* died?

Paula. *(simply)* That was just part of it.

Liz. Oh.

Paula. So I got me a garden hose, I mean a heavy-duty garden hose, and I took it down to the barn.

Cass. Why the barn?

Paula. 'Cause I like the barn.

Cass. Okay.

Paula. I went to the barn and found me a rafter and I threw the hose up over the rafter and made me a noose and everything.

Sherri Lee. Didn't you leave a note?

Paula. Uh uh.

Cass. Why not?

Paula. 'Cause it's bad manners to write a note without a return address.

Liz. Paula, sometimes your logic defies logic.

Paula. *(pleased)* I know.

Sherri Lee. Then what?

Paula. I climbed up on a bale of hay and put my head in the noose— *(PAULA is standing on the bench now.)* —and I told God that there was no way He could blame me for doing this. *No way!* I told Him it was all His fault because He made me fat. He did it and He oughta be man enough to take the blame for it. *(Beat)* And then I got scared and told Him I was just kidding. And then I jumped.

Sherri Lee. What happened?

Paula. *(disgusted)* The damned rafter broke! I was so fat the rafter just broke to pieces and I fell slap on the floor with the hose still around my neck.

CASS. That's pitiful!

PAULA. And about that time Mama came in and found me laying there with hay all up my nose and she like to has a heart attack. Screaming and crying—and then she started hitting me with the Weed Whacker.

LIZ. The Weed Whacker?

PAULA. Yeah. And she told me that suicide was against the law, and that if I ever *did* kill myself, she'd have me put away for life.

CASS. That's the saddest thing I ever heard.

PAULA. *(agreeing)* It was pretty grim—I mean, that was a big rafter and it wasn't even rotten or anything. It just couldn't stand the strain. I'm lucky I didn't pull the whole barn down.

LIZ. Oh, Paula. I can remember it and you weren't that fat.

CASS. *(matter-of-fact)* Liz, she was fat. She was *gross.*

LIZ. Cass.

CASS. Well, she was.

PAULA. *(hopefully)* Mama said I was big-boned.

SHERRI LEE. How fa—...*big-boned* were you?

PAULA. A hundred and ninety-three pounds.

SHERRI LEE. *(shocked)* Shit!

CASS. I told you she was fat.

SHERRI LEE. *(trying to comprehend it)* A hundred and ninety-three pounds!

CASS. All fat.

SHERRI LEE. A hundred and ninety-three pounds.

CASS. "Paula the Piglet."

LIZ. *(a warning)* Cass.

SHERRI LEE. How'd you do it, Paula? You're skinny. I

bet you don't even weigh...how much *do* you weigh?

PAULA. *(with pride)* Ninety-one pounds.

SHERRI LEE. *(amazed)* You lost a hundred pounds?

PAULA. *(evenly)* A hundred and *two* pounds.

SHERRI LEE. God. How?

PAULA. I just did it.

SHERRI LEE. You must live on a diet. *(to CASS:)* I bet she *sleeps* on a diet.

CASS. Are you kidding? You oughta see her in the lunchroom. Paula doesn't eat—she grazes. She eats that slop and *then* eats everybody else's and *then* goes back to ask for more.

PAULA. *(smiling)* I do not.

CASS. Y'all remember last week when we had those barbecued weenies with cheese melted on top?

SHERRI LEE. Vomit.

CASS. She ate seven.

SHERRI LEE. *(really curious)* Then how? How do you stay so skinny, Paula?

LIZ. Come on, Paula. Tell us your secret.

PAULA. *(enjoying this)* It's not secret.

CASS. Then tell us. *(suddenly)* Diet pills.

PAULA. Nope.

SHERRI LEE. Exercise!

PAULA. I don't exercise.

SHERRI LEE. Then how?

LIZ. How, Paula?

SHERRI LEE. Come on. Tell.

CASS. Tell us, Paula.

PAULA. I throw up. *(Beat)*

CASS. You're kidding. She's kidding.

PAULA. *(simply)* Nope. I vomit.

LIZ. Paula.

PAULA. I eat as much as I wanna eat. I can eat everything. Ice cream, Milky Ways, pies, cakes. I eat it and then I throw it up.

LIZ. Paula.

PAULA. I throw it up.

SHERRI LEE. That's nasty.

PAULA. *(defensive)* It it not. I can eat and eat all day long if I want to and then I just go in the bathroom and put my finger down my throat and that's that.

CASS. But, Paula...

PAULA. *What?*

CASS. Doesn't it, like, make you sick?

LIZ. You may have stumbled onto something, Cass.

CASS. *(realizing LIZ is making fun of her)* I'd rather be fat!

PAULA. *(insulted by this and suddenly very angry)* Well, you're not! You're not fat and you never have been fat, so you don't know, *you do not know* and you have no right to say that.

LIZ. *(trying to calm her)* Paula.

PAULA. *(losing control)* Nobody wants to be fat! You hear me? I don't care what they say—they pretend they don't care—but they hate it! And *I* hate it! And I'm not gonna be fat! I—WILL—NOT—BE—FAT! And I'll do anything I have to!

SHERRI LEE. But Paula, it's not good for you.

PAULA. Yes, it is! Yes. It *is* good for me! It's good for me and I like it. I do. I eat all I can and then I can't wait—*I can't wait* to get rid of it. I think about it all the time—all the time I'm eating, every bite, I'm thinking about throwing it up—about getting rid of it.

LIZ. Paula, calm down.

PAULA. *(PAULA'S voice grows louder, she is shaking.)* It's all I ever think about, y'all. All the time. And you know why? BECAUSE I DECIDE! *ME!* I decide exactly what happens and I'm the one that controls it all!

LIZ. Stop yelling, Paula.

PAULA. *(yelling:)* I'M NOT YELLING! *(Beat)*

SHERRI LEE. It can't be good, Paula. Just think what it's doing to your insides.

PAULA. *(agonized)* NOBODY CAN SEE THE INSIDES! DON'T YOU UNDERSTAND? I DON'T GIVE A SHIT ABOUT THE INSIDES! *NOBODY* GIVES A SHIT ABOUT THE INSIDES!

CASS. Paula...

PAULA. And as long as I don't have to see fat, I don't give a shit about *anything!*

SHERRI LEE. But Paula, you're gonna—

PAULA. JUST SHUT UP, SHERRI LEE! JUST SHUT UP YOUR MOUTH! YOU DON'T KNOW ANYTHING, YOU STUPID BITCH!

LIZ. Please sit down, Paula.

PAULA. *(not even hearing)* People are always trying to act like they know—telling me what's wrong with me!

SHERRI LEE. I didn't say—

PAULA. *(Has crossed to SHERRI LEE, who is sitting at stage left dressing table.)* You think you're real hot stuff, Sherri Lee. Ever since you moved here—ever since you breezed in last fall.

SHERRI LEE. That's not true, Paula.

PAULA. You're pretty...and you think because your eyes and your nose and your mouth come together in that cute way, you should get whatever you want! *(Beat)* And now you're Queen of Hearts. Well, so what? So what, Sherri Lee? That doesn't mean a thing. There's a new Queen of Hearts every year. There'll always be one—a *new* one. *(getting nearer SHERRI LEE)* Did you see all them women out there tonight? The ones that stood up in the audience? They were all Queen of Hearts , too. Every one of them was Queen of Hearts and just look at them now! THEY ARE STILL GETTING OLD! Look at my sister. Look at *her.* Queen of Hearts, married to a crummy preacher, all swelled up with a damned baby. NOTHING CHANGES, SHERRI LEE! *(with contempt)* Queen of Hearts doesn't mean shit! It doesn't mean shit, you hear? Queen of Hearts. Queen of Hearts! It's so stupid. *(PAULA reaches for the deck of cards on the dressing table and shuffles through it.)* Lookie here. *(She picks one.)* Here! Lookie here at this, Sherri Lee! This is the Queen of Hearts. The *real* one. See what she looks like? *(Pushes card at SHERRI LEE, who pushes it away.)* Look. LOOK! She ain't even pretty. She's the real one and she's ugly! Ugly and *fat!* *(PAULA giggles, trying not to sob.)* She couldn't win that contest out there in a million years. *See?* So it doesn't mean a thing, Sherri Lee. You hear me? QUEEN OF HEARTS DOESN'T MEAN ONE SHITTY THING! *(PAULA throws the deck of cards at her feet, but keeps the Queen, looking at it, crying, her hands shaking. Then she drops the Queen. She looks at it, crying. LIZ rises slowly, then tentatively takes a step toward PAULA, who seems to lean in LIZ's direction. SHERRI*

LEE sees this and breaks in.)

SHERRI LEE. *(standing)* **Paula?** *(PAULA glances back at SHERRI LEE, who steps in to PAULA. They meet halfway and embrace, PAULA crying and shaking, SHERRI LEE looking down at PAULA's head. All this should happen within seconds.)* I know it, Paula. I know it. *(For only a few seconds, SHERRI LEE looks up and over at LIZ with a glance of triumph. LIZ is angry, hurt, confused. She turns away.)*

PAULA. *(after a moment)* I, ummm— *(Pause)* —get um— I get a little carried away sometimes. *(Beat. A shaky smile.)* Mama says I'm excitable.

SHERRI LEE. It's okay. It is. I understand. *(After a moment, they break the embrace.)*

PAULA. Oh. Mama. *(She and SHERRI LEE part.)* I oughta get that over with, I guess.

SHERRI LEE. Are you sure? *(PAULA nods.)*

CASS. You're going out?

PAULA. Yeah.

LIZ. Tell her you were sick, Paula. She'll believe that.

PAULA. No, she won't. Boy, she's got a temper, too.

CASS. She looks so nice.

PAULA. Back when Daddy was living, he was so afraid of Mama. I mean he was *scared.* When they had a fight or something, he always made sure he told her he was sorry before they went to bed.

SHERRI LEE. That's sweet.

PAULA. No. Daddy was afraid if he went to bed with her still mad, he might wake up dead.

LIZ. *(laughing)* Oh, Paula.

PAULA. I'm serious, Liz.

CASS. God.

SHERRI LEE. Don't go out there, Paula.

PAULA. I got to.

SHERRI LEE. *(rising)* Want me to go with you? *(PAULA looks at SHERRI LEE with all the gratitude in her body. CASS' admiration is also clearly evident. LIZ is not taken in by this.)*

PAULA. *(a shy smile)* No.

LIZ. *(Holding out keys.)* Paula. *(PAULA takes keys and Exits, her posture admitting dread and defeat.)*

SHERRI LEE. We oughta do something to help her.

LIZ. She's scared.

CASS. What you think'll happen?

LIZ. I always thought Mrs. Burgess was a nice lady.

CASS. All mothers are nice ladies to other people.

SHERRI LEE. *(sitting across from CASS)* I know. My Mama's like that. She'd break her neck to be nice to anybody. Especially if it's like a stranger or something.

CASS. Mine, too.

SHERRI LEE. One time, a crippled man came to our house—selling magazines. He was real pitiful. Crutches and braces, you know? *(She looks at LIZ but LIZ turns away.)*

CASS. Yeah?

SHERRI LEE. *(Turns her attention to CASS.)* He asked Mama for a glass of water and she gave him one—ice water. Then, after he left, I remember walking through the kitchen and there was a big pan of water boiling on the stove—and the glass was in it. Boiling.

CASS. *(transfixed)* Really?

SHERRI LEE. She boiled that glass all day. I mean, she coulda said no, or she coulda given him a paper cup, but she gave him a glass glass—and then she boiled it.

Cass. God.

Sherri Lee. She never lets anybody use that glass. But whenever we move, she brings it. Two or three times, I've walked in the kitchen and caught her—just standing there with the cabinet door open—staring at that glass.

(PAULA Enters during the last few words of SHERRI LEE's story. LIZ is first to see her.)

Liz. What happened, Paula?

Cass. Paula? What did she do?

Sherri Lee. *(Crosses to PAULA.)* What did she say? Hey, Paula. Did she ground you?

Liz. Paula?

Paula. She's not there.

Cass. Huh?

Paula. She's gone. They're all gone. Except for Mrs. Robins—she's still counting the money.

Cass. They're probably waiting out in the car.

Paula. Uh uh. She's gone. Mrs. Robins told me. She said Joanie's having her baby. They all took off for the hospital. Mama and Aunt Christine and all of 'em.

Liz. When, Paula? When did they leave?

Paula. Before I went out in streetwear.

Liz. They weren't here thirty minutes.

Paula. *(hurt)* They didn't see me when I *did* go out. They weren't even there.

Liz. What luck! I can't believe it. Paula, nobody in the whole world could be this lucky.

CASS. It's great. Paula, you got it made.

LIZ. Yeah, because with the baby and everything, they'll be so crazy over at your house, they won't have time to worry about you getting kicked out of Queen of Hearts. Damn, Paula, you are so lucky that—

PAULA. *(furious)* THOSE-SON-OF-A-BITCHES! Those-son-of-a-bitches didn't even *see* me! Not a one of 'em. Why couldn't just *one* stay? That whole damned herd of cows here and not even one of 'em stayed to see me.

SHERRI LEE. *(sympathetically)* Hey, Paula. I know how you feel and—

PAULA. I HOPE THEY DIE! I hope they all die!

LIZ. *(dryly)* They will—eventually.

PAULA. RIGHT NOW! I hope they all fall down dead as shit! Joanie too! That fat sow son-of-a-bitch Joanie...I bet she did it on purpose. Yeah. She probably sat there and just strained herself stupid trying to make that baby get here.

LIZ. Paula, you're too loud. Mrs. Robins'll hear you and—

PAULA. I DON'T CARE! I DO NOT CARE! *(raging)* I hope Joanie's in labor for two whole weeks with that brat, and when it's born, I hope it's uglier than homemade sin! Yeah, I do! I hope it's ugly and...if Joanie breastfeeds it, I hope that baby's born with a full set of teeth!

LIZ. Paula.

PAULA. Yeah. And I hope it squalls twenty-four hours a day, and umm, when it grows, yeah, when it grows up, I hope it's— *(trying to think of something really awful)* —I hope it's a MORPHODITE!

Liz. *(trying to stop this with humor)* Come on, Paula. Don't hold it in.

Paula. IT'S NOT FUNNY!

Sherri Lee. Who's laughing? *(LIZ glares at SHERRI LEE.)*

Paula. *(running for the bottle)* I'm gonna get drunk again.

Liz. Oh, Paula. You don't wanna do that.

Paula. *(with bottle)* Yes, I do. *(She drinks.)* I sure do.

Cass. Paula.

Liz. Come on, Paula.

Paula. No.

Liz. *(trying to take bottle from PAULA)* Paula, listen to me a minute. Okay?

Paula. I want my bottle.

Liz. I know how you feel.

Paula. *(a whine)* Give me my bottle.

Liz. Paula, just—

Paula. *(twisting away with the bottle)* NO! Now just leave me alone!

Sherri Lee. *(stepping in, trying to divert her)* Paula? Hey, Paula. *(PAULA looks at her. SHERRI LEE is removing her crown. LIZ stands back, watching.)* You wanna try this on?

Paula. Huh?

Cass. Yeah, Paula. Try it on.

Sherri Lee. *(holding out crown)* See what it looks like.

Paula. *(forgetting her bottle)* I'd feel silly.

Sherri Lee. Think how silly I felt. Here. *(She puts crown on PAULA's head.)* Just see. There. Tah-dah.

CASS. Yea! Great, Paula. *(PAULA rushes to mirror.)*

PAULA. How do I look?

CASS. Like real royalty.

SHERRI LEE. Like Miss Alabama.

CASS. Like Miss America. *(CASS begins singing the "Queen of Hearts" theme. Then LIZ joins in. SHERRI LEE pulls a single rose from her bouquet and give it to PAULA, then hums along with LIZ and CASS. PAULA is caught up in it and, halfway silly and halfway serious, walks around—smiling, waving, and blowing kisses to her imaginary fans. The GIRLS sing three or four lines of the song, then they all laugh. SHERRI LEE snaps a photo of PAULA.)*

PAULA. It's kinda tight. I don't think I'd like being Queen full-time. I might get headaches.

SHERRI LEE. Oh, yeah.

PAULA. When Joanie won, she *slept* with her crown on.

CASS. Really?

PAULA. Uh huh. And she wanted to wear it to church the next day and Mama let her do it, too.

CASS. To church?

SHERRI LEE. You're kidding. Really?

PAULA. Yeah, because it was Easter and all and people dress up more on Easter.

SHERRI LEE. Didn't everybody stare?

PAULA. No. They probably just thought it was her halo.

LIZ. *(using this as a way back into the conversation)* Hey Paula, that was pretty good.

PAULA. *(surprised at herself)* Yeah. Yeah, it was, wasn't

it? *(She laughs and extends bottle to CASS.)* Here. Have a drink on me. Everybody have a drink on me.

CASS. Yeah! *(She drinks.)*

LIZ. *(Beginning a song, CASS and PAULA join in.)*
GIVE A CHEER!
GIVE A CHEER!
FOR THE GIRLS—
WHO BREW THE BEER,
IN THE BASEMENT
OF OLD
WINSTON HIGH!

(CASS passes the bottle to LIZ. CASS and PAULA continue singing as LIZ drinks. Next, LIZ intends to pass the bottle back to PAULA, but SHERRI LEE steps in and intercepts it. As SHERRI LEE steps in, she takes up the song.)
THEY ARE BRAVE
THEY ARE BOLD—
AND THE LIQUOR
THEY CAN HOLD
IS A STORY
THAT'S NEVER
BEEN TOLD.

(LIZ is aware of what SHERRI LEE has done, but continues singing. SHERRI LEE smiles at her.)
GOT DRUNK LAST NIGHT
AND GOT DRUNK THE NIGHT BEFORE.
OH YEAH WE'RE GONNA GET DRUNK TONIGHT
AND THEN WE'RE GONNA GET DRUNK SOME
     MORE!

(The song ends as the bottle is passed around again.)
GIVE A CHEER!

GIVE A CHEER!
FOR THE GIRLS
WHO BREW THE BEER,
IN THE BASEMENT
OF OLD
WINSTON HIGH!

(The GIRLS laugh and applaud themselves. CASS takes a huge drink and SHERRI LEE snaps a photo of her.)

PAULA. *(to SHERRI LEE:)* I've heard y'all sing that on the band bus.

SHERRI LEE. Yeah.

PAULA. Going to football games. *(suddenly)* I don't have a way home. Y'all, I don't have—

LIZ. You can ride with me and Cass. We're going to my house.

PAULA. *(relieved)* Okay. *(She has an idea.)* You come too, Sherri Lee.

SHERRI LEE. *(eagerly)* Okay. Yeah!

PAULA. *(remembering)* Oh. Your boyfriend's still coming. *(to LIZ and CASS)* Let's wait. Can we stay with Sherri Lee till Mark gets here?

SHERRI LEE. *(Crosses to her overnight case and begins packing.)* Well y'all, um, he's not coming.

CASS. Why not?

SHERRI LEE. He's just not.

PAULA. But you said he was. You said he was working late at U.P.S. and he was on his way.

SHERRI LEE. Well y'all...see, I just made that up.

CASS. Why? Where is he really? *(playfully)* Did y'all have a fuss?

SHERRI LEE. No, Cass. He's not anywhere. I made

him up.

CASS. Huh?

LIZ. Well that's crappy, Sherri Lee. Why?

SHERRI LEE. *(shrugging)* I don't know. I just did.

CASS. *(still not quite believing it)* But everybody thinks you're engaged. I heard the teachers talking about giving you a shower.

SHERRI LEE. *(turning away, packing again)* I know.

CASS. You showed me a picture of him. I saw Mark's picture. In that brass frame. I saw him.

SHERRI LEE. That picture was in the frame when I bought it.

CASS. Huh?

SHERRI LEE. *(directly to CASS)* It's a picture of some model, Cass. It came in the frame.

PAULA. But your ring.

SHERRI LEE. Mama and Daddy gave me this.

CASS. *(stunned)* Damn. It's like—like a death or something. One minute you're engaged to Mark and then next thing you know, he's not even real. It's like somebody died, Sherri Lee.

SHERRI LEE. *(uncomfortably flippant)* God, Cass, would you feel better if we said a prayer or something?

CASS. No, I just...but *why?*

SHERRI LEE. Cass, I already—

CASS. Why would *you* make up a boyfriend?

SHERRI LEE. I guess because I don't have one.

CASS. Yeah, but...God, all the boys here would...you could take your pick, Sherri Lee. You—

SHERRI LEE. How do you *know,* Cass?

CASS. How do I know? God! Don't you have *mirrors* at

your house? *(Half-laughs.)* I mean, look. You're like a movie star or something.

PAULA. Yeah. A movie star.

CASS. The boys are crazy about you. Every boy in Ag class wanted you to be Queen of Hearts. They love you. *(incredulous)* And you make up a boyfriend in Mobile? God, I can't—

SHERRI LEE. Cass, the first five weeks I was here, not one boy asked me out.

CASS. Oh, I don't—

SHERRI LEE. *Not one single boy.*

PAULA. But, Sherri Lee, at majorette tryouts—

SHERRI LEE. *(evenly)* At majorette tryouts, they yelled and hollered and whistled and I got picked feature twirler. That's right. But not one boy ever asked me out.

CASS. *(amazed)* I can't believe this.

SHERRI LEE. So, I made up a finacé. *(fingering her ring)* Mark Patterson. *(Tries to laugh.)* My true love. At least he gave me an excuse for sitting home on weekends. *(She pauses and looks at them.)* I *know* it sounds awful. It's the worst thing I've ever done. It's terrible, isn't it, y'all?

PAULA. *(trying to convince herself and the others)* No. No, I don't think it's so bad. I mean, I think it's kinda funny. It's a good joke. Like...Liz, it's like what you did.

LIZ. *(absently)* What?

PAULA. It's like what you did that time.

LIZ. What are you babbling about, Paula?

PAULA. *(hurt)* I'm not babbling. *(Turns to CASS.)* Am I?

CASS. *(stepping in to help)* She means what you did at

that Valentine banquet. About making up a date and all.

Liz. It's not the same.

SHERRI LEE. *(intrigued)* What? When did Liz make up a date?

CASS. *(trying to draw them all together again)* Oh, it's a great story. Tell her, Liz. *(LIZ says nothing. CASS tries again.)* Liz was going to this Valentine banquet and she— Liz, *come on.* Tell Sherri Lee about—

Liz. *(refusing to be budged)* It's not even close to the same thing.

PAULA. Well, yes it is. Just think about it, Liz. Just think—

Liz. Just shut up, Paula. My story is nothing like what she did. There's nothing similar about it.

CASS. But Liz—

Liz. She *lied.* She made up lies just for the hell of it— because she thought it would be fun. Her "hobby."

CASS. No, Liz. It's just the same as—

Liz. I did it because I had to. Because I couldn't get a date and I was ashamed. *(Beat)* I was thirteen years old. I was ashamed.

SHERRI LEE. Well, I'm ashamed. I'm *eighteen* and I'm ashamed. *(LIZ looks away.)* I am. I don't even have a date for the prom. I was gonna have to pretend—

CASS. *You* don't have a date for the prom?

SHERRI LEE. No. And I—

Liz. If she doesn't have a date, it's her own fault.

CASS. Liz—

Liz. Because she's a fake. And boys don't like fakey girls. It's her own fault. And that's why she'll be sitting home on prom night. Only *real* girls get asked to the prom. *(CASS' reaction to this is not lost on SHERRI LEE. LIZ is immediately sorry, but it's too late.)*

SHERRI LEE. I said I was ashamed. And I am.

LIZ. I'll bet.

SHERRI LEE. I *had* to do it, y'all. Making up Mark Patterson and all that. I mean, just think about it. I'm the only girl in the whole senior class who doesn't have a date.

CASS. No, you're not.

SHERRI LEE. What?

CASS. I don't, either.

PAULA. But Cass, I thought Eddie Akers was—

CASS. No. I don't have a date, either. *(CASS is now aligned with SHERRI LEE. LIZ sees this happening and attempts to end it.)*

LIZ. Cass—

SHERRI LEE. Really, Cass?

CASS. Yep.

SHERRI LEE. Looks like we're both in the same fix, then.

CASS. Yeah. But I don't care.

LIZ. *Cass?*

SHERRI LEE. Me, either. Hey, Cass, you know what we should do? We could go together and—

LIZ. Stop it. Just stop this right now, Sherri Lee.

SHERRI LEE. Stop what?

LIZ. This is shitty. What she's doing is shitty. Can't y'all see?

SHERRI LEE. Liz—

LIZ. Every single thing she's done for a whole year— ever since she came here, it's shitty! Acting like she's somebody else—pretending to be stuck-up and so religious and everything. That's sick.

PAULA. But Liz—

LIZ. *(very upset, seeing her friends slip away)* There's something bad wrong with a person who'd do things like that. Don't y'all see? What kinda person would—what kinda *mind* would think of doing those things, just for the hell of it?

CASS. *(bravely)* To tell the truth, Liz, I don't see anything all that—

LIZ. *(near tears)* Listen! You hated her! You hated her guts so bad you couldn't see straight—ever since she came to Double Springs—up until a few minutes ago, anyway. That's pretty strange, Cass, don't you think?

PAULA. But Liz, it wasn't really *her.* She was just pretending she—

LIZ. You hated her too, Paula!

PAULA. I never hated her. I never *did.*

LIZ. Oh hell, Paula. You're such a wimp.

CASS. Hey, now Liz—

LIZ. *(exploding)* Shut up, *Lezzie!* You— *(LIZ regrets this the second it is spoken. CASS turns from her, very hurt. Then LIZ whispers hoarsely:)* Cass—?

PAULA. *(after a moment)* I never hated you, Sherri Lee. I never did hate you. *(to LIZ:)* I don't hate people.

LIZ. *(coldly)* Show Sherri Lee your majorette routine, Paula.

SHERRI LEE. What?

LIZ. *(directly to PAULA)* Yeah. Paula did this really great half-time show before you came in. She was good, too. Feature twirler. But she made us call her "Sherri Lee."

SHERRI LEE. *(realizing)* Oh. Well. I don't care.

LIZ. *(turning and crossing away)* Forgive and forget. How sweet.

CASS. What's your problem, Liz?

LIZ. I don't *have* a problem!

CASS. Then what's the matter?

LIZ. *(appealing to CASS, a bit desperately)* How do you know she's not doing it again? *(SHERRI LEE smiles innocently.)*

SHERRI LEE. Doing what, Liz?

LIZ. How do you know this isn't another act? Who *are* you, Sherri Lee? Do you even know? Somebody else from Mobile or wherever you lived before that? Who are you being *right now?*

SHERRI LEE. Liz, come on.

LIZ. This buddy-buddy shit. What is this? What are you doing this for, Sherri Lee? *Why?*

SHERRI LEE. Because I like y'all.

LIZ. Oh, please.

SHERRI LEE. I do. I like all y'all. And I wanna be around y'all. This is my senior year and I'm getting ready to graduate and I don't have one single friend.

LIZ. *(crossing to opposite dressing table)* I'm crying buckets.

SHERRI LEE. Give me a chance, Liz.

LIZ. *(straightening up)* I'm going home.

SHERRI LEE. Out of everybody in this school, I wanted *you* to like me. I wanted *you*, Liz. I—

LIZ. Stop it, Sherri Lee! Just stop it. The Queen has her ladies-in-waiting— *(Looks to CASS and PAULA.)* —so you can just stop. *(She turns and puts her hands on the table again, looking down. Here SHERRI LEE becomes almost obsessive.)*

SHERRI LEE. It's the truth, Liz. I swear to God. I've always wanted a friend like you—

LIZ. *(softly)* No.

SHERRI LEE. —and I want to hang around with you and—

LIZ. *(louder)* No.

SHERRI LEE. —and I want us to be *best friends* and—

LIZ. *(exploding, turning to face her)* NO! *(They stare at each other. Then, softly:)* No. *(CASS and PAULA are looking at SHERRI LEE's back. They can't see her face, but we can, and there is something very disturbing here. Her expression doesn't fit her words at all. Just listening to her, her voice is very sincere, but her face is mocking, insolent, triumphant. LIZ sees it.)*

SHERRI LEE. If you'd just listen, Liz. We could be friends. We could. If you'd just give me—

LIZ. *(breaking away from SHERRI LEE's near-hynotic gaze)* I DON'T WANT TO! I DON'T *WANT* TO GIVE YOU A CHANCE, SHERRI LEE! Don't you understand me? I *don't want* to like you. I don't. So leave me—leave *us all* alone. We don't like you, Sherri Lee, so just *leave us alone.* *(Pause. Then, to CASS and PAULA.)* Come on, y'all. It's time to go. Past time. Paula, check and see if those lights back there are off. *(No one moves.)* Well, hell, come on. I don't have all night to screw around here. *(pleading)* Let's go! *(She starts out. No one else moves.)* Are y'all coming or not? *(a touch of fear)* Y'all?

PAULA. *(almost sympathetically)* I don't think so, Liz.

LIZ. *(regarding PAULA)* Well, why the hell not? *(Beat)* All right. Stay then. Come on, Cass.

CASS. No.

(A car HORN blows outside. PAULA reacts slightly.)

LIZ. *(confused and angry)* Well what... *(Looks at them all. Very upset.)* Well shit. *(surrendering here, desperately trying to hold on to CASS and PAULA)* All right. Okay. *(A deep breath. This is extremely difficult.)* Okay, I'm sorry. I'm sorry, Sherri Lee. I'm sorry. You wanna—you wanna come too? *(SHERRI LEE looks up at LIZ, enjoying watching LIZ squirm. SHERRI LEE smiles, but doesn't answer.)* Is everybody happy now? Huh? Okay. Good. *(urgently)* Now let's go.

(The HORN sounds again.)

PAULA. *(rising, more to herself than LIZ:)* No.
LIZ. *(near tears)* Why not? Why—?

(HORN sounds again, several times, rapidly.)

PAULA. *(crossing quickly to Exit)* Mama. That's *Mama!*
LIZ. *(following her to door, as PAULA Exits) Wait!* I'll— I'll take you where you wanna go. Paula?

(HORN sounds again.)

LIZ. Who the *hell* is making all that racket? *(LIZ is very frustrated now.)* The keys. I had those keys, Cass. What did I do with—? *(CASS picks up the keys.)*
CASS. Here. Right here.
LIZ. Okay. Good. Yeah, just go and lock that door back—

(CASS tosses the keys at Liz. LIZ doesn't try to catch them and they fall against her body and to the floor. LIZ looks down at them, then to CASS, who is almost as surprised as LIZ. We see hurt on LIZ'S face. CASS looks as if she wishes she could call the keys back. Then LIZ looks to SHERRI LEE, who has been watching all this with amusement. SHERRI LEE returns LIZ's gaze with a slight smile. Hold on this just a moment, then a NOISE from offstage. It is PAULA knocking and shouting.)

PAULA. *(offstage)* Y'all? Hey y'all. Let me in! The door's locked! Hey, y'all? *(CASS, who has been looking from LIZ to SHERRI LEE, uses this as an escape and rushes out with keys.)*

CASS. *(Exiting)* I'm coming! *(SHERRI LEE and LIZ stare at each other.)*

LIZ. *(hoarsely)* Sherri Lee. Stop it. *(Beat) Please* stop it.

SHERRI LEE. *(Rises and crosses to LIZ.)* What's the matter, Liz? We were having fun.

LIZ. Sherri Lee, please—

SHERRI LEE. And you're not having fun now.

LIZ. No. It's—

SHERRI LEE. *(Turns and crosses away.)* I guess nobody likes to lose.

LIZ. *(suddenly afraid)* Sherri Lee, let's just—we'll *all* go to my house. Okay? *(SHERRI LEE has the Polaroid in hand.)* You wanna do that? Huh? We could do that and—

SHERRI LEE. *(Brings the camera up to her eye.)* Smile, Liz.

LIZ. *(really scared)* Sherri Lee! *(SHERRI LEE brings the camera to chest level.)* What—what are you *doing?*

SHERRI LEE. *(simply)* I'm winning.

(She brings the camera up. At the same time, CASS and PAULA enter. SHERRI LEE snaps the photo of LIZ.)

PAULA. It's my Aunt Christine! Joanie had a boy!

CASS. Yeah, a boy!

SHERRI LEE. *(putting camera down and going to them)* That's great, Paula. You're an aunt. Aunt Paula.

PAULA. *(Considers this, decides she likes it.)* Aunt Paula. Yeah. *(Laughs.)* Well, y'all, Aunt *Christine's* waiting outside to take Aunt *Paula* to the hospital. Anybody wanna go?

SHERRI LEE. Oh, I do.

CASS. *(not looking at LIZ, who is standing, watching numbly)* Yeah. Let me get this stuff.

SHERRI LEE. Oh, yeah. Me, too. *(The three GIRLS begin gathering things, LIZ watching.)*

CASS. Don't forget your purse, Paula.

SHERRI LEE. Or your *bottle,* Paula.

PAULA. *(laughing)* Yeah, my bottle!

SHERRI LEE. *(taking down her extra gown)* This is mine.

LIZ. *(Grasping at straws, her tone is one of defeat, but she tries her best to hide this.)* Well, hey y'all, wait just a minute. Okay? And then we can all get outta here. Okay? *(CASS, PAULA and SHERRI LEE all stop their motions and look at LIZ as she continues.)* Uh, wait and let me go and lock this door and we'll *all* leave. Okay? Just one minute, okay? *(She starts off with the keys.)* It'll just take me a minute, y'all.

(She exits. No movement for two or three beats as the GIRLS look

*at each other. The the HORN blows twice. It brings the GIRLS
back into action.)*

SHERRI LEE. *(with her make-up case)* All this is mine.
CASS. Need some help?
SHERRI LEE. *(as CASS crosses to her)* Yeah.
PAULA. Oh. *(Begins removing crown.)* Sherri Lee. Your
crown.
SHERRI LEE. No, no. You wear it for a while. I crowned
you Aunt Paula. You wear it.

(This pleases PAULA. HORN blows twice again.)

PAULA. She's driving Mama's truck!
CASS. A truck!
PAULA. Yeah.
SHERRI LEE. Oh, let's all ride in the back, y'all!
CASS. Yeah, like a parade! And Sherri Lee can blow
kisses and we can wave at everybody! *(As the other two girls
chatter, SHERRI LEE uses the Polaroid photos to arrange a subtle
tableau for LIZ. She places the photos on the wooden bench—then,
almost as an afterthought, adds the single red rose that she presented
earlier to PAULA. All this should happen within seconds and
should go totally unnoticed by CASS and PAULA. Then SHERRI
LEE jumps back into the conversation.)*
PAULA. *(raising bottle)* And drink!
CASS. Yeah!

(HORN sounds again.)

PAULA. She's gonna leave us!

CASS. Not me!

SHERRI LEE. Me, either. I'm sure not walking home in this gown! *(She runs out with her things.)*

PAULA. Well, what about me in this majorette suit? *(PAULA sees that SHERRI LEE has forgotten her trophy. She crosses to it and picks it up.)* Sherri Lee! You crazy! You forgot your trophy.

(She and CASS laugh and start out with their things, when they are stopped by LIZ's voice from off-stage.)

LIZ. *(off)* Okay! All locked up and ready to hit the road. Hey, y'all, I got a great idea. Why don't we all go to the prom together? *(Her voice is begging and CASS and PAULA recognize this. It is decidedly not the LIZ they thought they knew. This is someone else—someone weaker. Beaten.)* Yeah, all four of us could go together. Just us girls. *(CASS and PAULA are ashamed for LIZ. They look at each other as they listen.)* It'll be fun. We'll get drunk at my house and then go to the prom. *(CASS and PAULA start out, humiliated for LIZ.)* Okay? What do y'all think?

(PAULA Exits, but CASS stops in the doorway, looks back, then switches off the overhead LIGHTS. She raises her chin decisively, then rushes out.)

LIZ. Wouldn't that be fun? Hey, y'all? *(Her voice grows louder as she nears.)* Cass? *(She Enters at a half-run, stopping near center-stage, looking around the darkened room.)* Paula? *(It takes only a second or two for it to sink in. LIZ recognizes what has happened. She is hurt, ashamed and confused. She crosses down to the rose and photographs that SHERRI LEE left behind, picks up the photos from underneath the rose, then speaks with a knowing half-whisper:)* **Sherri Lee.** *(All this occurs within moments.)*

(Count two. With the toe of her shoe, she nudges the deck of playing cards that PAULA dropped to the floor, still holding the photos of herself and PAULA and CASS. LIZ drops to her knees and begins picking up cards. Then we hear the TRUCK MOTOR rev up, immediately followed by the sound of the THREE GIRLS outside, happily singing as the TRUCK pulls away. LIZ reacts, turns her head to that direction—listens.)

GIRLS.
GIVE A CHEER,
GIVE A CHEER,
FOR THE GIRLS
WHO BREW THE BEER,
IN THE BASEMENT
OF OLD
WINSTON HIGH. (etc.)

(After a moment of listening, LIZ brings her focus back in—to herself—to the photos she has in her hands. She sits back on her haunches, puts the photos back on the bench—touches the rose— then returns to picking up the cards. The TRUCK SOUND, the singing and the remaining LIGHTS start down slowly. It is here we see from LIZ's attitude that she is hurt, but not destroyed—not defeated, but resigned. And as the singing and the sound of the truck fade away, we watch LIZ methodically, and very, very neatly, reassembling the deck.)

BLACK

QUEEN OF HEARTS THEME

You wished upon a falling star,
Kept waiting for the day
    that dream would take you far.

You always knew it in your heart,
That dreams can come true,
They just need a start.

So meet
    the lovely Queen of Hearts—
The style and the grace
    our lovely Queen of Hearts

See the smile on her face
It's true—
    your dreams follow you.

(Repeat verse as needed.)

101

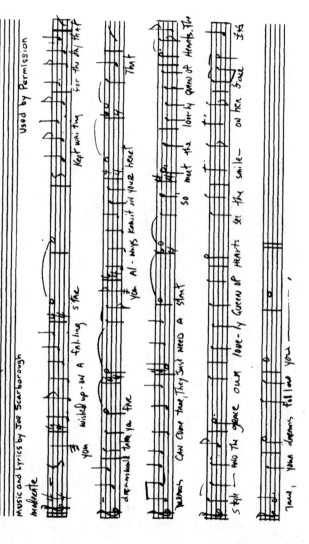

"Queen of Hearts - Theme"

Music and Lyrics by Joe Scarborough

Used by Permission

GIVE A CHEER! GIVE A CHEER!

Give a cheer!
Give a cheer!
For the girls—
Who brew the beer,
In the basement
Of old
Winston High!

They are brave,
They are bold—
And the liquor
They can hold
Is a story
That's never
Been told.

Got drunk last night
And got drunk the night before.
Oh yeah we're gonna get drunk tonight
And then we're gonna get drunk some more!

Give a cheer!
Give a cheer!
For the girls
Who brew the beer,
In the basement
Of old
Winston High!

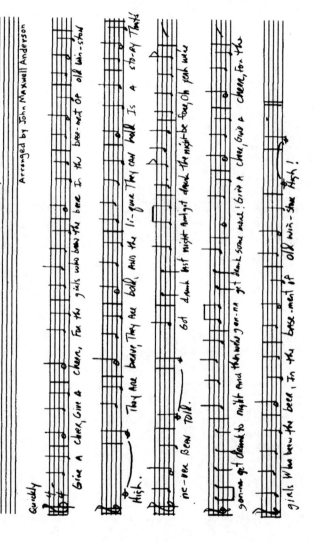

COSTUME PLOT

ACT I

LIZ — Large man's shirt, bell-bottomed jeans, tennis shoes

CASS — T-shirt* imprinted with "WCHS" on front and "Pep Squad" on back, bell-bottomed jeans, tennis shoes

SHERRI LEE — Expensive evening gown (possibly white), heels, small chain necklace, diamond ring, rhinestone earrings, number "13" glittered in silver on a paper heart

PAULA — Hideous green diaphanous gown (perhaps chiffon) with a long gauze-like cape built-in, ugly wristwatch, green high-heels, gaudy earrings, a paper heart with the number "39" glittered in silver

ACT II

LIZ — The same as Act I

CASS — The same as Act I

SHERRI LEE — The same, plus a rhinestone crown and a large sash (ribbon) that reads: "Queen of Hearts 1976"

PAULA — 1950's majorette uniform* majorette ankle-boots, a large band-member's hat (called a busby), same wristwatch

*The school colors at WCHS are purple and gold.

PROPERTY LIST

ACT I

Cheerleader Pom-pons (purple and gold or purple and white)—these are half-way visible in a box labeled "Cheerleaders." The box rests atop the lockers. In or near this box, several Majorette's Batons.

Other boxes labeled "W-Club," "Band," "Homecoming," etc.

Miscellaneous make-up supplies scattered about the locker room: brushes, combs, rollers, curling irons, lipsticks, eye shadows, mascaras, hair sprays — all this strewn throughout, especially on the two dressing tables and the table in front of the lockers.

Miscellaneous "pageant debris" — cotton balls, tissues, Q-Tips, also fast-food cups, containers and bags, etc.

Discarded casual clothes here and there — blouses, shirts, jeans, shoes, a row of purses on the floor (Paula's purse is here, also), overnight cases, garment bags, even an ironing board and iron.

Make-up mirrors (the lighted, portable variety) at each table, also blow dryers at each table.

Paula's pass from Mrs. Taylor — pinned to the back of her gown — should read: "Please excuse Paula, she is drunk."

Sherri Lee's pass — "Sherri Lee has permission to go backstage" and signed "Mrs. Taylor." Also her earrings pre-set on any table.

Sherri Lee's extra gown, on a hanger.

Cass has a deck of playing cards when lights go up.

ACT II

Sherri Lee has a dozen red roses, a ribbon sash reading "Queen of Hearts 1976," a trophy, a Polaroid camera (functional).

Liz has a set of keys from Mrs. Taylor.

A box of chocolates pre-set with Sherri Lee's other things.

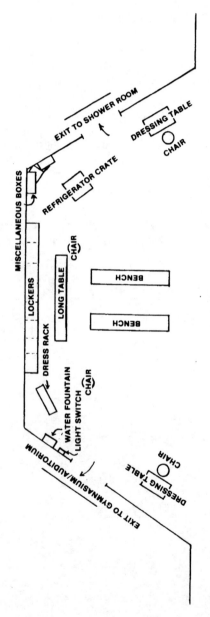

SCENE DESIGN
THE REAL QUEEN OF HEARTS AIN'T EVEN PRETTY